D1601657

Beyond Limitations

The Power of Conscious Co-Creation

Stuart Wilson and Joanna Prentis

PO Box 754
Huntsville, AR 72740
479-738-2348 or fax 479-738-2448
www.ozarkmt.com

For permission, or serialization, condensation, adaptions, or for our catalog of other publications, write to: Ozark Mountain Publishing, Inc., P.O. Box 754, Huntsville, AR 72740, Attn: Permissions Department.

Library of Congress Cataloging-in-Publication Data
Wilson, Stuart - 1937 -
Prentis, Joanna - 1943 - 2020
    "Beyond Limitations" by Stuart Wilson and Joanna Prentis Channeled material from an angelic being on consciously creating a better reality and moving beyond your limitations.
1. Creating Reality   2. Conscious Co-Creation   3. Channeling   4. Alariel I. Wilson, Stuart, 1937 -   II. Prentis, Joanna, 1943 -   III. Title
Library of Congress Catalog Card Number: 2009941814
ISBN: 978-1-886940-40-6

Cover Artwork: enki3d.com
Cover Layout: enki3d.com
Cover Model: Makaylia Thornton
Book Design: Julia Degan
Book Set in: Times New Roman, Papyrus
Published By

OZARK
MOUNTAIN
PUBLISHING

PO Box 754, Huntsville, AR 72740
800-935-0045 or 479-738-2348 fax: 479-738-2448

WWW.OZARKMT.COM
Printed in the United States of America

Table of Contents

Part One: Beginnings

1   Alariel   3
2   The Big Question   6

Part Two: Personal Reality Creation

3   The Principles of Being   11
4   Core Beliefs   18
5   The Basic Mechanism of Reality Creation   23
6   The Limiting Protocols   26
7   The Influence of Others   33
8   The Principle of Sequence   36
9   Seven Levels of Reality Creation   38
10 Manifestation and Timing   40
11 Reincarnation and Choice   43
12 Timelines and Lifelines   46
13 Overview of the Creative Process   49

Part Three: The Bigger Picture

14 Three Key Relationships   55
15 The Seven Steps of Co-Creation   59
16 Instantaneous Creation   64

Part Four: A Time of Change

17 From Religion to Spirituality   73
18 Personal and Planetary Changes   76
19 The Evolution of Channeling   81
20 The Crystal Children   92

Part Five: Awakening to the Real

21 The Three Realities   99
22 The Way of Light   104

Part Six: New World, New Consciousness

23	The Advancement of Consciousness	111
24	Transition and the Big Questions	114
25	A Comparison Between 3D and 5D	122
26	Beyond Limitation	131
27	Learning and Growing	134
28	The Arc of Spiritual Development	137

Part Seven: Conclusion

| 29 | An Emerging Understanding | 141 |
| 30 | Summation | 144 |

Further Reading	147
Acknowledgments	151
About the Authors	153

Part One:

Beginnings

1

Alariel

Joanna writes: It all began in 1988 when, with my daughter, Tatanya, I set up the Starlight Centre in the West of England, a Centre focusing on healing and the expansion of consciousness. Two years later, Stuart joined us to help with the development of the Centre, and he writes about this period:

> *It was inspiring and fascinating but also exhausting! A stream of visitors came in to the Centre, mainly from the United States and Australia, but some also from Europe. We had an amazing and mind-expanding time sitting at the feet of internationally respected spiritual teachers and workshop leaders. What I remember most about this time was the big gatherings when our friends came in to share a meal and talk about our experiences and all the changes that were happening in our lives. It was a wonderful time, full of joy and laughter, and the special events — like Anna Mitchell Hedges sharing her crystal skull, a Magnified Healing workshop with Gisele King, and the two fire-walks led by Essassani — were simply magical !*

When I went on to train as a past life therapist with Ursula Markham, this gave the Centre a new focus, and a whole cycle of past life work began. Although we explored a number of historical periods, our work took a new direction through the

3

gradual accumulation of seven past life subjects who had lives two thousand years ago in Israel. Most of these people were Essenes, and they told a remarkable story that ran parallel with the New Testament account, but also contained some striking differences. Although it was not our intention at that time to write a book, the result of our work eventually produced enough material for a book called *The Essenes, Children of the Light*, which was published in March 2005 by Ozark Mountain Publishing in America.

Our past life work continued, now with subjects coming from as far away as Germany, thanks to our friend Isabel Zaplana who proved to be a brilliant translator. And when seven subjects had completed their regressions, we had enough information for another book. It was when we were working on this second book that we made our next breakthrough. We were exploring one of Stuart's lives on Atlantis as an architect called Anquel, when a question which he could not answer was referred to one of Anquel's contacts called Alariel. This angelic being told us that he spoke for a group of twelve angels who work with the Order of Melchizedek. (The full story of our first contact with Alariel is given in Chapter 8 of *Power of the Magdalene*, published in December 2008 by Ozark Mountain Publishing.)

We realized from the beginning that this contact could be a unique opportunity for us, and Alariel's insight and knowledge gave our second book a depth which a past life process alone could not have provided. At one point, we asked Alariel to tell us the limits of this process of dialogue.

Joanna: Are there any questions you are forbidden to answer?
Alariel: There are some questions that we choose not to answer, and these come into three categories:
There are Words of Power which give access to control frequencies in the angelic world. We obviously would not reveal these.

There is information which forms part of the research which other groups on Earth are well advanced on, and will soon reveal — we would not wish to "steal their thunder."

And finally, there are concepts so far beyond your present understanding that they would disorient you and cause you distress. It is not a kindness to reveal this type of information and we will not do so.

Having said that, there is still a vast amount of information for you to explore.

Joanna: We appreciate that these communications are a great opportunity. Why has this opportunity been given to us?

Alariel: When you sent your first book out into the world, it opened up a doorway of Light, a portal leading to future possibilities. These dialogues are one of the results of opening that doorway. The reward of work is more work, but it gets more interesting as your consciousness develops!

Our relationship with Alariel changed and evolved over a period of time, and gradually through this contact we came to see him as a channeling source of remarkable depth and clarity. Some of the information we received surprised us, and much of it stretched our imagination and challenged us to expand our awareness. Our dialogues with Alariel were beginning to transform our work, and we became aware that we might be able to access information that went way beyond anything which was currently available.

2

The Big Question

When the work on our second book was almost completed, we began to approach the question which had been at the back of our minds for some while. It is certainly a big question — many people might say THE big question — but we decided to ask it in a simple and direct way.

Joanna: How do we create our own reality?
Alariel: Reality creation is very complex, and a short answer would only cause confusion. Please be patient while we address — in outline at least — all the aspects of this subject so that you can gain a real understanding of what is involved.

There are seven Fundamental Questions about reality creation that must be addressed before the whole process can be understood. These Questions are:

1 Where is personal reality created?
2 When does the process of reality creation start?
3 What empowers you to create a reality?
4 How is this creation process achieved?
5 What can limit the process of reality creation?
6 Who can influence your life experience?
7 How can the process of personal reality creation best be summarized?

It will take some time to unpack the answers to these Questions, but as they are so fundamental and go to the very heart of personal reality creation, they are worth pursuing thoroughly.

Before we set out to address these Questions, it is necessary to ask:

When is this reality being created?

The key supplementary question here is:

Are you creating this reality before or after 2012?

Your whole planetary cycle is drawing to a close, and when a planet nears the point of Transition something remarkable happens. The Earth is approaching Transition around — and we stress "around" — the year 2012, and it's about to move upwards in vibrational frequency. What that means in practice is that everything — including your own consciousness — will start to focus in a higher, lighter and clearer way. All the human beings remaining on planet Earth will leave behind the heavy, rigid, over-structured processes that really don't work any more, and become subtler, lighter, more responsive and creative beings.

This change in your consciousness is being focused by the Transition, and as part of that Transition you are now being given the opportunity to see the process through which you have been creating reality for yourselves up to this point. In other words, you are starting to penetrate the veil so that you can begin to live consciously rather than unconsciously.

You've been creating your own reality at a unconscious level for thousands of years: this is part of the experience you set up, the game you decided to play. That's fine and in a sense your ability to function in a veiled state has served you well. But when a planet goes into Transition, it challenges the sentient beings upon it to try to understand how they have been manifesting their lives.

Much of the information required to bring this understanding has already been communicated, but much also remains to be presented, so the communication process must continue. It is important to stress that this communication process is now a big team effort, and many minds are at work to present the information in a number of complementary ways that support each other and combine to give the complete picture. As you absorb this information, you will begin to move beyond the veiled state and into a new level of consciousness in which you can start to live as fully-aware beings.

The veiled state has contributed to your learning and growth, but now it is time for the veil to be set aside and clarity accessed on the whole process through which you create your own reality.

Part Two:

Personal Reality Creation

3

The Principles of Being

Alariel : We will describe the process of creating personal reality under a number of headings which we shall call "Principles of Being." This whole process is about manifestation, about Being, about the way you project yourselves down into a physical life on this planet.

We begin with the first of the seven Questions:

Fundamental Question 1 :
Where is personal reality created?

Here the key question is:
How much reality are you creating?
Are you creating the reality of the entire Universe?

Clearly not, so you're creating the reality of some area smaller than the whole Universe. The next question is:
How much smaller?

The truth is that you are creating the reality of a little world that surrounds you, a small bubble of experience which is focused on you and accompanies you wherever you go. The existence of these little individual worlds of being accounts for people having such different experiences even when they are in the same location. Some people perceive life as joyful, safe and loving, and others see it as dangerous and full of anger and hatred. If these are the qualities which dominate their consciousness, then this is what will permeate their bubble of reality and color their experience. Your bubble of reality is the focus of your life experience, the crucible within which you create your own reality.

We can now give a summary of the Principle of Containment:

> Each human being carries around
> his or her own little world,
> like a small bubble of experience.
> This is the crucible within which
> you create your own reality.

We would stress that reality creation is a complex and subtle process and the mechanism underlying it has never been fully understood up to this point. Some of the basics have been perceived, but until now, human beings have been too highly veiled for a complete understanding to develop. However, this veiling was necessary so that you could experience life here to the full. Think of it like playing a game: if you start the game as a conscious and fully-aware Master of that game you'll simply be demonstrating your Mastery. It will be a repetition for you and not a learning process.

The learning process is exciting: there are new discoveries to be made and challenges to overcome. As you wanted both the challenge and the excitement, you decided to accept the veiling process and play the game of living on planet Earth in this particular way. When we say "you," we mean you at the soul level when you set up this game a long time ago. You, humanity, set up the game in this way and now collectively you as humanity want the veil to be drawn back. You want to see what is really going on and understand the whole of what is happening to you and not just a tiny part of it. These communications, and others like them which are emerging from other groups, are part of the process of drawing back the veil.

Joanna: You speak about excitement and challenges. Do we really want the challenges too?

Alariel: The challenges are just as important to you as the excitement, the triumphs and celebrations. Through the problems that test the limits of your abilities, you extend those abilities. With the help of these challenges, you are able to learn and grow.

Fundamental Question 2:
When does the process of reality creation start?

Your beliefs, especially those foundational beliefs which are called "core beliefs" become a key element in this whole process. A core belief has both an emotional and a mental aspect in it, and that makes it quite different from any casual belief which you may happen to hold for a time, something that passes through your consciousness and is soon gone. The dual nature of a core belief reflects the way it emerges in your consciousness: it starts as a persistent thought, moves through the stage of being a gut-feeling, and finally settles down into a core belief.

The energy in your consciousness is expressed as thoughts, feelings and beliefs. These thoughts, feelings and beliefs — both conscious and unconscious — merge together to build your view of the world, your Picture of Reality. The whole process of reality creation starts when you develop a Picture of Reality. It is important to understand that your Picture of Reality arises from the very core of your being and reflects your perception of the Universe. It is supported by your life experiences and your programming when you were a child — which is a time when you were particularly open and would easily absorb the beliefs and attitudes of your parents, role models and teachers.

Your Picture of Reality shows what you expect to happen. As what you expect to happen does tend to happen, this becomes a closed loop of self-justifying results, a self-fulfilling prophecy. A pessimist expecting difficulty and setbacks will tend to find them, just as an optimist expecting good things will find good things happening in his or her life.

The Picture of Reality is an important part of the mechanism by which you create your life experience. Your thoughts, feelings and beliefs are the energy you project out into the Universe. When you project your energy, that energy attracts similar energies which are vibrationally compatible with your Picture of Reality. In this way, the Universe matches what you send out, so that the loving and peaceful get peace and love, and the angry and violent get anger and violence. This process of attraction lies at the heart of reality creation because like always attracts like.

We can now give a summary of the Principle of Instruction:

> The thoughts, feelings and beliefs
> forming your Picture of Reality
> go out into the Universe
> as a signal, an instruction,
> and this instruction attracts
> similar energies to you
> because like attracts like.

Fundamental Question 3:
What empowers you to create a reality?

Many people feel that they do not have the power to make major changes in their own lives, and for that reason could not possibly be creating their own reality. What they don't realize is that their thoughts, feelings and beliefs simply provide the energy to send a signal out into the Universe. It is the Universe which amplifies this signal by adding all the energy required to rearrange a personal reality and manifest a new life experience.

If people only knew that they have the power to ask the Universe to change their reality, they would understand that they are not weak and helpless victims of circumstances, but empowered Children of the Light exercising their birthright as Creator-Beings. A Being of Light is empowered to ask the Universe because the Universe is itself made of Light. So in a sense, when you send a signal out into the Universe, you are sending a signal into the essence of your own being, and it is because the Universe recognizes you as a Child of Light, as being one with itself in essence, that it obeys your request. Thus, manifesting a reality is fundamentally you and the Universe being as one, and moving as one, and this is the real secret of your own nature and your own power.

We can now give a summary of the Principle of Amplification:

> The instruction you send out
> is amplified by the Universe,
> which supplies all the energy required
> to create your reality.

Fundamental Question 4:
How is this creation process achieved?

You live in a kind and compassionate Universe, and the Universe demonstrates that kindness by linking together the outer world of your experience and the inner world of your consciousness. The Universe is constantly rearranging itself within the bubble of your experience to create a reality that reflects your consciousness.

The Universe accepts what is in your consciousness without any attempt to edit or judge it. It accepts this as a symbol of what you wish to experience, your "home state of being" as it were, and it tries to reproduce this vibrational quality, this miniature "home" around you wherever you go.

So what is in your consciousness is the key to the whole process. If there is struggle and difficulty and suffering in your consciousness, then the Universe will reproduce all that around you, but if there is love and peace and abundance, the Universe will reproduce that instead. Remember that it's a kind Universe, but it's also an automatic system and it does not edit the contents of your consciousness. It does not say, "Oh, they don't really want THAT do they?" No, it just gets on and reproduces around you whatever happens to be in your consciousness. This is how the inner and outer worlds are linked.

Now, all this is very difficult for modern industrialized societies to understand because they don't have any elements in their culture which would help them to make sense of it. However, in a traditional shamanic society, they would understand that the inner and outer worlds are indeed linked, and although they may not see all the mechanism of reality creation, they have at least got a head start in understanding the basis on which it works.

In modern Western cultures, people just don't see this connection between the inner and the outer worlds, so they tend to project judgment and blame outwards onto other people. They criticize and blame their partner, their children, their boss, their rival, their enemy — indeed anyone except themselves for the difficulties and disasters that befall them. And because they find it impossible to explain why some people enjoy health and wealth and others clearly do not, they rely upon the idea of chance or luck.

Joanna: Many people believe in the existence of luck - would you like to comment this?

Alariel: If chance or luck ruled your lives, this would mean you lived in a cruel and random Universe, where things happened for no reason at all. This is not the Universe that we recognize. We see the Universe as essentially loving and kind, a place where justice is always done in the long run. Isn't that the sort of Universe that you would like to be part of?

But to return to our theme: the key to the whole process is what goes on in your own consciousness. The product of your consciousness is the energy which you are continually feeding in to the Universe. The Universe keeps pace with the changes in your consciousness, so that your outer world is rearranged to reflect these changes.

We can now give a summary of the Principle of Rearrangement:

> Your outer world is a reflection
> of your inner world.
> The Universe maintains this connection
> by constantly rearranging itself
> within your bubble
> to create a reality
> which keeps pace with the changes
> in your consciousness.
> That reality, unfolded through time,
> becomes your life experience.

4

Core Beliefs

Joanna: You have talked about core beliefs. These seem to be a key part of the process, so could you explain them further please?

Alariel: At the heart of your process of personal reality creation, lies your core beliefs. What these core beliefs build up in your mind and your emotional body is a framework, a map of reality as you think and feel it to be. This is not a single idea, but a whole structure put together in your consciousness over a period of time. You start unconsciously building this structure during your childhood, and keep adding to it during the early adult years. By middle age, it is usually quite firm and well established, the central focus of beliefs being supported by a number of perspectives, values, prejudices and opinions.

It is unusual for this structure to change very rapidly, although that can happen when the individual experiences a big breakthrough, like a religious conversion. However, it is much more common for the belief structure to change and evolve slowly as life experience undermines some long-cherished belief, and new perspectives start to creep in.

A core belief is much more powerful than even a persistent thought: it is a statement about life which is so much a part of your being that it may seem dangerous even to question it. If there are fixed stars on your horizon, reassuring certainties that you can always rely on, these are your core beliefs.

Core beliefs often have a powerful and sweeping generality about them which cuts through any attempt at logical analysis. The belief simply states: "This is how the Universe is for me."
A good example of a core belief might be:

Life will always be a struggle.

Another might be:
Rich people can never be spiritual.

Whenever you encounter any beliefs with "always" or "never" lurking inside them, your suspicions should be aroused. Because human experience is constantly changing, "always" or "never" do not seem to be accurate descriptions of it. In a process of constant change, anything is possible. So if your parents were really poor, there is no need for you to be poor — unless of course, your core belief is:

I will always be poor.

If you sincerely believe this in the very core of your being, THAT is the signal you'll be sending out to the Universe, and the kind Universe, thinking you actually WANT poverty, will manifest this for you! So be careful what core beliefs you allow into your life, especially those which reflect your beliefs about yourself.
Ultimately, limitations are not imposed upon you — they flow from your own consciousness and are only valid and powerful when accepted by you. For example, if you believe that you must accept and live within your problems, then those problems become impossible for you to solve. But what is happening here is that your belief is stopping you from solving the problems.

You continually make choices and are open (or closed) to opportunities and options in line with your core beliefs. You expect the world to deliver a life experience in line with your beliefs, and through the process of reality creation, this is what happens. Another way of putting this is to say that you get in life what you expect to get. Thus, the doom-laden depressives are always right in expecting difficulty and disaster, while the sunny optimists are also right in expecting good things and happy times. Both doom and happiness arrive on schedule, but they arrive because your belief system expects them and is the original seed of their creation.

Through the core beliefs you hold in your consciousness, you are the author of your own happiness, or your own misery. Your consciousness is a creative instrument of enormous power, but like any tool of great power, you need to treat it with respect and learn how best to use it.

Above all, your everyday reality is an indicator of your core beliefs. If you want to know what your core beliefs are, just examine your life experience. What does the world look like to you? Do you live in a loving, creative and abundant world, or a world full of limitation, anger and violence? It's the same planet that you're all living on, but your diverse belief systems can give a wide variety of life experiences upon it.

If you investigate your core beliefs (as demonstrated by your life experience) and change those beliefs into something much more positive and more aligned with your aspirations and your dreams, the results can be dramatic. Instead of doing this, most people fill their consciousness, not with what they aspire to, but with whatever they fear and dread. If you sit there constantly focusing on your house being repossessed, then that will happen, and it will be caused by you focusing on what you DON'T want.

Your conscious mind is equipped to examine both the outer world of experience and the inner world of the psyche. And as you begin to examine both these worlds, and compare them, your ability to change your reality consciously will increase. Identify and weed out false beliefs — ideas that seem to be true, but are really not. A certain amount of detachment is needed for this process of exploring your core-beliefs to be effective. In particular, you need to become detached about your parents' values and beliefs. Only then are you really free to construct beliefs of your own.

This process of self-knowledge opens the channel to your own inner power. Do not inhibit your thoughts and feelings — become aware of them and change them where necessary to make them more positive and helpful in the process of reality creation.

Say to yourself:

My life is my creation:
I made it and I can change it.

And be aware of how big a step you have taken here, since this is both a statement of empowerment and also a conscious realization that you are in charge of your own life, and therefore, fully responsible for it.

Joanna: As many core beliefs are formed in childhood, we may not be aware of them at the conscious level. Someone, for example, who as a child has seen his home go up in flames might be left with the feeling that this might happen again, and that could result in all kinds of anxiety-related patterns of behavior.

Alariel: It's quite true that many core beliefs from childhood can cause anxiety patterns, and that the real nature of these beliefs may be invisible to the person concerned. In other words, you can see the behavior, but not the ultimate cause of that behavior.

Joanna: And how could this behavior be changed?
Alariel: This is entirely an individual question, and no "one size fits all" solution can hope to be effective. Many of the new therapies that are now emerging focus on ways to address the behavior patterns that come from core beliefs.

5

The Basic Mechanism of Reality Creation

Alariel: We are now in a position to survey the whole Basic Mechanism of reality creation. First of all, it might be helpful to repeat the Summaries which outline the four parts of the process:

> The Principle of Containment
> Each human being carries around
> his or her own little world,
> like a small bubble of experience.
> This is the crucible within which
> you create your own reality.
>
> The Principle of Instruction
> The thoughts, feelings and beliefs forming
> your Picture of Reality
> go out into the Universe
> as a signal, an instruction,
> and this instruction attracts similar energies to you
> because like attracts like.
>
> The Principle of Amplification
> The instruction you send out
> is amplified by the Universe,
> which supplies all the energy required
> to create your reality.

<u>The Principle of Rearrangement</u>
Your outer world is a reflection
of your inner world.
The Universe maintains this connection
by constantly rearranging itself
within your bubble
to create a reality
which keeps pace with the changes
in your consciousness.
That reality, unfolded through time,
becomes your life experience.

So here we have the four stages within the Basic Mechanism:

1   Containment: You create your own reality within a small bubble of experience.
2   Instruction: Your Picture of Reality sends out an energy-signal as an instruction to the Universe.
3   Amplification: The Universe amplifies the signal and supplies the energy needed.
4   Rearrangement : The Universe rearranges itself within the bubble to create a new reality.

So this is essentially a fourfold process of:

Containment
Instruction
Amplification
Rearrangement.

Here you have an outline of the whole Basic Mechanism of reality creation, and seeing a summation of it like this emphasizes the central importance of consciousness. Consciousness is not a mere sideshow, an isolated component within your system of being. In truth, the whole of the reality creation process is initiated by your consciousness, and without consciousness, no such process would occur. Consequently, it is not an exaggeration to say that:

> The entire manifestation of your reality
> flows from your consciousness,
> and is shaped by it.
> Through the working of your consciousness,
> you project your inner dream
> onto the outer stage of the world,
> where you can inhabit your dream
> and play a role within it.
> Consciousness makes and projects the dream,
> and can make and project another dream,
> a better reality,
> another opportunity to learn and grow.

6

The Limiting Protocols

Alariel: So now we come to the factors which limit the way you create your own reality.

Fundamental Question 5:
What can limit the process of reality creation?

We have described the Principles which combine to make the Basic Mechanism of personal reality creation. However this Mechanism is modified by Limiting Protocols which set the boundaries on what you can achieve in the way of creating your own reality:

1. Karma
Karma is a complex subject with many branches to it, and we shall content ourselves here with a very broad outline to set it within the framework of reality creation. The whole system of karma is administered by a host of Recording Angels who work with the Akashic Records and advise souls when in the Interlife planning the next incarnation on the Earth. The Akashic Records are an automatic system recording the thoughts, words and actions of all sentient beings. This is not a piece of technology added on to the Universe, but an integral part of the functioning of the Universe itself. By thinking, speaking or acting, you imprint energy upon the higher frequencies of the Universe, and this energetic trace becomes the basis of a complete record of the soul in its journey down into matter and up again into the Light.

There is personal, group and planetary karma. Personal karma is the positive or negative merit acquired by the soul in its pilgrimage through a number of lives. Group karma distinguishes various groups, ranging from a small community right up to a nation in size. Finally, there is planetary karma, the combined karmic impact of human life on the Earth. All these elements — personal, group and planetary karma — interweave within your life experience to give that experience a remarkable depth and complexity, and distinguish one human being from another. You may be born in the same area at a similar time and within the same family as another person, but if your karma is different, you will have a different experience of life and quite different perceptions based on that experience.

Karma may not prevent you from achieving a particular goal in creating a certain reality, but it may slow the process down or make the goal more difficult to achieve. This difficulty may mean that the goal is not attainable within a single life, as it may require effort spanning several incarnations.

2. Vows

A vow of poverty taken when you had a life in a monastery, convent or ashram would certainly have an impact on any kind of reality you tried to create which had a financial aspect to it, until the point that this vow is released. A further instance which would limit the level of abundance in your life is a vow never to acquire real wealth until you had repaid a certain karmic debt. This is another example of karma acquired in a past life limiting the reality you may be trying to create in this life. If you are having real problems with abundance, it would be a good idea to look at possible past life causes that may be affecting the reality creation process here and now.

Other vows taken in past lives can influence your life in other ways. Vows of celibacy taken in religious lives may make it difficult to sustain meaningful relationships, and a vow of obedience can make it difficult to stand up to any authority figure, even when they are acting unreasonably.

A vow is essentially a fixed limitation in the sense that it remains in place until it is released by an act of firm intent. For example, the deliberate speaking of a form of words to set aside the vow. This is a different situation to other limitations in your life, which can be more fluid and less fixed. For example, in the case of a limiting core belief, this starts to release and dissolve automatically from the moment you begin to understand it and the part it has played in influencing your life. By recognizing the limiting core belief, in effect you reject it, and it starts to weaken from that point on. This does not apply to vows. Whether you understand and recognize them or not, they still remain in force until you release them by using a deliberate form of words, uttered with intent.

3. Cultural Environment

No human being exists in a vacuum, and every person lives and moves within the environment of their own culture. This environment is not limiting in the sense of a handicap or diminishment, but it does point you in a certain direction, making some values easy to absorb and others easy to deny. Every culture has its favorite areas of operation, and its habitual prejudices and fixed opinions. Some of these prejudices and opinions may influence your values and even creep into your core beliefs, so you need to be aware of what your culture really represents.

Every culture has illusions about itself, and tends to portray itself as better, nobler and more effective than it is. So it's your job to probe behind these illusions and discover what your culture is really like. You have to avoid sentiment and be tough-minded to do this, but it may give you some vital clues about weaknesses in your core beliefs that are culture-related and may have been limiting you without your knowledge. Every human being is both a product of their culture and a child of their time, at any rate until they are aware of their own real nature and enter their empowerment. And the concept of a "child of your time" leads us on to the next aspect of the Limiting Protocols: the Historical Context.

4. Historical Context

You do not create your life in isolation, separate from everything happening upon your planet. In living, you move through a historical period and absorb the Spirit of the Age. This colors many of your attitudes, and may influence your beliefs. You cannot escape from the shared experience of human evolution, and by being part of this collective, you are part of the healing of the greater whole.

Yet you can also carve out your own destiny within this collective, choosing the positive even when you are surrounded by the negative, and insisting upon expanding your consciousness and increasing your capacity for joy and love. Nor should the historical context be seen always as a negative force, for it can give you a springboard into the expression of your own greatness. This is particularly true in the case of creative artists, in whose lives the Spirit of the Age can play a vital part. Talented musicians like Beethoven would be impressive in any era, but only when great talents unite with the Spirit of the Age can an immortal genius arise. The full extent of that genius marks the degree to which the artist is able to resonate with the Spirit of his or her Age, and express its ideals and its unique quality and energy.

5. Soul Override

The soul will veto and prevent any activity or line of development in two areas:

(A) It will block your efforts and prevent you from achieving your goals in an area if that line of development would not be for your highest good, or would make it impossible for you to learn a lesson chosen for that life.

(B) It will block any line of development which is likely to be self-destructive, unless self-destruction is the chosen lesson for that life.

The soul chooses in the Interlife before an incarnation begins the specific lessons which it wishes the incoming personality to learn during this life. When you enter an area of reality creation which leads directly towards one of these lessons, you can expect rapid progress and a good deal of help from the soul. The soul will do all that it can to facilitate this process so that the lesson is learned quickly and easily. But it will also block lines of development that take you away from areas where your lessons can be learned.

So here you have the complete outline of all the Limiting Protocols, and the result of these Protocols is that boundaries are set on the reality you can create. This does not mean that you are prevented in absolute terms from ever achieving these aims, but you may have to wait for a better time if you find yourself continually blocked along one line of development.

This is where the ability to tune in and get clear inner guidance is so useful. If you can find out the reasons you are being blocked, it can be much easier to accept the situation and change your goals. Even if the underlying reason is not clear, it can still be an advantage to get a clear energetic signal from the soul that this chosen line of development is not for you at this time.

Maybe the soul is trying to save you from some disaster that would flow from the achievement of your goal — like the development of a major ego problem. Or perhaps you have climbed to the top of this particular mountain in some past life and — although you're still drawn powerfully to this area of activity — there's no point in repeating the pattern. Continual blocking is always a sign that something fundamental may be wrong with your goals and aspirations. When you get into this position, it is always a good idea to tune in to the soul through meditation or prayer, or any other method that works for you such as dreamwork or oracle systems, in order to get some clarity on the situation.

Joanna: Why are these limitations called "Protocols?" It seems a strange word to use.

Alariel: Because they form the core of an agreement drawn up between the soul and the soul's angelic advisers in the Interlife. These are the rules of the game you have decided to play in a third dimensional setting. Although the personality is not conscious of these rules, the soul is very much aware of them.

Joanna: These Limiting Protocols do seem to make reality creation more complex.

Alariel: Yes, but if you are to embrace the whole truth of reality creation that cannot be avoided. Sometimes the impression is given that you can just reorient your consciousness in a positive direction, and keep saying positive affirmations, and then you can be sure of having good experiences and an easy life. In other words, it is suggested that you can simply pull the levers of universal power and never have to probe into your inner world. However, a superficial approach seldom works in the long run. When you understand the part played by core beliefs, and vows from past lives, you will realize that it pays to find out exactly what is going on. It is tempting to take a simplistic view of reality creation, but it is much wiser to examine your inner world and deal with the energies involved.

Joanna: I accept that, but the Limiting Protocols do restrict our lives.

Alariel: Please do not think that the Basic Mechanism of reality creation is entirely positive, whereas the Limiting Protocols are entirely negative: that would be a gross over simplification. People who do a lot of self-work and read (and hopefully apply) self-help books — especially those who focus on the power of positive affirmation — may have the impression that their thoughts, feelings and beliefs have been so transformed that they are now entirely positive. If they think that, they are unaware of the total process of reality creation.

Let us assume that their self-work has been thorough and effective and they've turned round their thoughts, feelings and beliefs so that these are indeed positive. Yet this is only the first element in reality creation: thoughts, feelings and beliefs at the conscious level. What about all the energies at work at the unconscious level? They cannot be aware of these because by definition, they are beyond the scope of the conscious mind, but unconscious thoughts, feelings and beliefs can sabotage even the most determined efforts.

The existence of this unconscious element will always mean that there may be unexplored negativity (especially from past lives) that you are not aware of. But there are also some invisible aspects of your life that are positive influences, like the soul overriding lines of development that are self-destructive or not for your highest good.

Even the vows you have taken in past lives may have served you at that time, and are simply acting as limitations because you haven't got round to releasing them yet. In the process of finding out about them and releasing them, you may learn important lessons about your past, and about who you are.

We can now give a summary of the Principle of Modification:
The Limiting Protocols
modify the operation
of the Basic Mechanism.

7

The Influence of Others

Joanna: Although we may create our basic reality, surely other
*   people also have an impact on our lives?*
Alariel : Yes, and that brings us to the next Question:

Fundamental Question 6:
Who can influence your life experience?

The people who are present in your world can influence your
life experience. They are there either because they are playing
roles you wish to be played in your life-drama, or because they
have some karmic connection with you from past lives. As both
your present life-drama and your karmic links are the result of
choices you are making, or in the past have made, in a sense you
are totally responsible for the impact that other people have upon
your life experience, although the personality — which lacks the
long view of things — would probably not agree with this
assessment.

What we have here is a series of overlapping dramas, like a
number of plays that are running simultaneously. You are playing
roles for other people, and they are playing roles you need to see
in your drama. All these overlapping dramas are linked by
consent — at the soul level everyone has consented to be in this
multi-drama process, so there are really no victims here, only
volunteers.

If you exclude karmic connections in your life, then your
chosen level of vibration becomes a key element in selecting the
people who inhabit your world. And if, for example, you raised

3

the vibration of your consciousness, you would attract different people who would bring more positive and beneficial elements into your life.

This process works in very specific and practical ways. People whose consciousness vibrates at the same level are magnetically attracted to each other, whereas a big difference in vibrational level will push people magnetically apart. This means, for example, that you will be magnetically drawn to people who match your patterns and share the same energy-channels in the emotional field. They will reinforce the working of these energy-channels in your astral field, mirroring and intensifying your experience and thus helping you to move beyond it. The same process occurs at the mental level, as they reinforce your opinions and prejudices until you outgrow them. When you choose to become aware, change and move on, you will find that you attract more people who will help you achieve your goals. At the same time, those old friends who were impeding your progress will drop out of your experience.

You also have a hand in keeping the characters in your life in place, at least those who have no karmic connection with you. And by becoming aware and making conscious choices, you control the flow of many of the actors into (and out of) your life-drama. If you expand your consciousness, rise in vibration and make empowering choices, the non-karmic personnel in your life will change, and even your relationships with those you are linked to in karmic ways will become more positive and more supportive of building the kind of reality you would like to experience. In this way, consciousness changes everything, even the impact that other people have on your life.

When you look at the actors in your life-drama, they can all be contributing to your growth process, but they may be doing this in very different ways. The encouraging parent, the inspiring teacher, the creative collaborator, the supportive friend, may be positive and empowering in obvious ways, but do not be too quick to label the more challenging actors in your drama as "negative." For example, some "expert" who blandly tells you that you (or your child) will never succeed in a given area may provide exactly the spur you need for you to prove how wrong they are. Some of your past-life friends may choose to play this kind of role, so that they can "rattle your cage" and challenge you when that's exactly what's needed to move you forward.

We can now give a summary of the Principle of Change:

> The actors in your life-drama
> reflect choices you have made,
> and when your consciousness changes,
> your cast of actors will change too,
> although the karmic connections
> will remain until the link
> between you is resolved.

8

The Principle of Sequence

Alariel: So now we come to the final Question:

Fundamental Question 7:
How can the process of personal reality creation best be summarized?

We have been studying the individual elements within the reality mix, and the sub-processes which operate within the total process of personal reality creation. That process can now be viewed as a whole, revealing the chain of events which occurs when all the components work together. By viewing the drama of reality creation in this compressed and telescoped way, the sequence underlying the whole process is revealed:

We can now give a summary of the Principle of Sequence:

> Your consciousness determines
> your thoughts and feelings;
> your thoughts and feelings determine
> your core beliefs;
> your core beliefs shape your Picture of Reality.
>
> Your Picture of Reality produces an energy which,
> amplified by the Universe and
> modified by the Limiting Protocols,
> creates your reality.

That reality, unfolded through time,
creates your life experience.
If you wish to change your life experience,
start by changing your consciousness.

This summary emphasizes the importance of consciousness as the first cause from which everything else flows. It points to consciousness as the seed of the whole manifestation process, the inner cause generating outer effects in the world around you.

What this means in practice is that the levers of power are firmly in your hands. By changing your consciousness, you can set in train a process that will change your life experience. This may take a little time, so don't look for immediate results. What you can be sure of is that results in your outer world will certainly come if you change your consciousness.

9

Seven Levels of Reality Creation

Alariel: Having described both the Basic Mechanism and the Limiting Protocols, we are now in a position to consider the levels on which Personal Reality Creation operates:

The Basic Mechanism of Reality Creation:
1   Thoughts, feelings and beliefs at the conscious level
2   Thoughts, feelings and beliefs at the unconscious level

The Limiting Protocols:
3   Karma
4   Vows
5   Cultural Environment
6   Historical Context
7   Soul Override

The whole structure — the creative flow and the boundaries that restrict that flow — is part of a learning framework that you (at the soul level) have set up for yourself. From that perspective, even the limitations and restrictions can be seen as teachers illumining your path to self-mastery.

By living on the Earth, you are learning that the physical world is the result, the creation, of thought and feeling. This means that your experience is the product of your mind and your spirit, and not a random series of events. This is very different from a conventional perspective, but it has major implications in the direction of releasing you from limitation and empowering you.

It enables you to take complete responsibility for everything that happens to you — the whole manifestation of your life. This empowers you to make changes in that life and create another kind of reality for yourself, and it reassures you that you are the master of your own destiny.

10

Manifestation and Timing

Joanna: Many people are finding this kind of information on creating reality pretty heavy going, and these ideas quite difficult to grasp.

Alariel: We appreciate that some of these ideas will seem very strange to the average person. Remember that it may take a little time to grasp these principles, and there is obviously great pressure on time in your Western culture.

You can certainly create some realities here and now, within a matter of days or weeks, but other dreams may take longer to manifest. Having dreamed a big dream, you may think you're ready for it to manifest, when in fact that would only create chaos in your life because you're not prepared for it yet. When you've worked to develop your skills and prepare your consciousness, and you really ARE ready, the dream will manifest, but then the timing will be right. A really big dream will bring you opportunities, but also big challenges. Being the central focus — the focalizer and main vision-holder — of a big dream is like being the Chief Executive of a large company, and it requires skills in handling people, organizing, delegating, decision making, prioritizing and thinking in structural ways.

The timing of your dream is really important. If you are too far ahead of your time, very few people will understand what you're trying to do, and vital areas of support may be missing.

You might, for example, have been able to design a computer system in 1750, but the technology to support your design would not be available for another two hundred years. At the other extreme, trying to manifest a dream that was attuned to an earlier era, simply repeating with variations what has been done before, will not generate much support or interest.

The dreams which make a real difference in the world are those which are perfectly attuned to the Spirit of their Age, the dreams whose time has come. Optimizing the timing of your dream within your Historical Context is quite an art, but if you can manage to do this the Historical Context ceases to be a limitation and instead becomes a source of support and empowerment. Any well-timed dream can expect the way to be cleared for it and many eager hearts and minds will welcome its arrival. These timely dreams resonate with a deep need felt by many people, and they will often burst into full flowering very rapidly. Look at how quickly the Berlin Wall came down. People had been dreaming of taking it down for a long while, and suddenly the energy built up to a point where nothing could stop it — and at that point, everything happened very quickly.

Here we are touching on areas of personal reality creation which prefigure the way in which a much higher form of reality creation works — a form that we will describe at a later point in these dialogues. But even within personal reality creation, you can experience amazing results with well-timed dreams. These lead into quite a different situation which transcends the normal rules and challenges you to accept new levels of liberation and empowerment:

> When you're surfing a wave of energy
> which has built up in many hearts and minds,
> be prepared for miracles!
> These are the magical moments
> when the walls crumble,
> the barriers dissolve,
> and peace breaks out against all the odds.

41

These are the moments when the mind surrenders
and the heart takes over,
and what was impossible yesterday,
becomes the living reality of today.

11

Reincarnation and Choice

Alariel: The whole system of creating personal reality is underpinned by the process of reincarnation. This provides a sequence of lives in which reality creation can occur. If you had only one life upon this planet, your opportunity for creating a range of realities would be very limited.

Joanna: Some people say that the lives we have on Earth are entirely random, just the incoming soul being attracted to this couple of parents or that couple, just the law of attraction with no planning behind it. What is your view about this?

Alariel: From our perspective, there is a universal system of planning and choice. We have seen the souls of countless sentient beings, in this galaxy and in other galaxies, conferring with their angelic advisers in the Interlife to plan their next incarnation. The angels who administer the records of the soul's journey will advise on karmic links with appropriate parents, but first of all, the soul chooses which lessons it wishes to learn in the life that is to come. This choice will often determine the appropriate country or culture to facilitate that learning process. So at the soul level, you choose your cultural environment, your country and your parents.

Joanna: But some cultures, especially in middle eastern and Asian countries, still restrict and limit what a woman can do, and how much education she can have. Surely no one would willingly choose to be born in such a restrictive and limiting environment.

Alariel: The soul wishes to have the widest possible variety of experiences, in order to extract the maximum benefit from life as a human being, and learn everything that a physical environment can teach. Some of these experiences are expanding and liberating, and some are restricting and challenging, but that is all part of the broad spectrum of human life.

Choice is the overlighting principle of the reincarnation process, and balance is its objective. The whole system of reincarnation works towards balance, the balancing of easy lives with more difficult ones, free lives with more restricted ones, lives as a man with lives as a woman, and so on.

Joanna: Some people say that souls are always born as female, or always born as a male. Is this true?

Alariel: Having studied reincarnation records throughout this galaxy, we see a very different pattern. Some people have had only a few lives on this planet, especially if they were originally Star Beings who came to Earth with a special task, and these individuals often remain in one gender throughout their few lives. But if we take the great majority of human beings, the usual gender rotation is between 9 and 12 lives, followed by 9 to 12 lives in the opposite gender. Some souls do have a quicker rotation cycle, and have 4 or 5 lives as a man and then 4 or 5 lives as a woman. In some cases, the batches of lives do exceed 12 in one gender, but we have never come across a case where a soul has had as many as one hundred lives as a man, or one hundred lives as woman.

If you think about it, you can understand why this should be so. The whole reincarnation process is a system of balance, and an excessive concentration of lives in one gender would make that balance more difficult to achieve.

Joanna: So the soul is always trying to move towards balance in planning a sequence of lives?

Alariel: Yes. Take the example of a brilliant intellectual who has overstretched himself at the mental level in one life. He may wake up in his next incarnation to discover that he has become a simple person with a very limited understanding. However, he may still have a rich and satisfying life at the emotional level, even if his intellectual capacity is very limited.

This is a good example of the balance being maintained by the soul, with a life taken to extremes in one direction being balanced by the next which offers a very different experience, but a fundamentally balancing and healing one.

12

Timelines and Lifelines

Alariel: A timeline is a trace left in linear time by an event or cluster of events. Major and minor timelines interweave to make a complex tapestry of manifestation which various angelic groups study and react to. We say "react to" in the sense of facilitating and enabling the development of a promising timeline which emerges through the incarnation of a special soul. This may serve to clear the way for the soul to be able to do important work as an agent of change, work which is vital for the spiritual or cultural evolution of that civilization.

A lifeline is a trace left in linear time by the expression in manifestation of a soul. As angels, we watch the ebb and flow of lifelines in this and in other galaxies, and we take the long view. Above all, we are cautious before labeling any life as a success. We see large numbers of lifelines, but we would regard only a minority of these lives as being totally successful. Where apparently successful lives lived on the world stage involve the harming of a number of other beings (human or animal), we would regard these lives as relative failures because of the heavy karmic burden involved in recompensing (in future lives) all those involved. In comparison, a life which is lived modestly in obscurity making no headlines, but practicing many small acts of kindness, we would regard as a major success.

But here we want to focus mainly upon timelines. Groups of angels in the Interlife observe the development of timelines in several ways, one of these being to see them displayed through a system of projected light. Try to visualize this process as it is seen by these angelic observers. They are watching major timelines, identified by geometric symbols, weaving together with minor timelines, which are identified by color-coding. Displaying the timelines in this way shows the patterns start to develop as energies interact and outcomes emerge. These outcomes may be uncertain over the course of a few months, or even years, but when a whole century of development is reviewed over a few hours the picture often becomes clear.

Visualize these displays of light in your mind. Major timelines form broad highways of light and establish the sweep of history like the main themes of a piece of music, while narrower light-roads formed by minor timelines intervene briefly like moments of melody which enrich the pattern but are soon replaced by others. Movements of change and patterns of development ebb and flow like tides, and with the weaving together of all these timelines, the whole tapestry can be seen unfolding in great complexity.

Joanna: With all this complexity of timelines, is it still possible to predict the future with any accuracy?

Alariel : Future prediction is difficult because of the complex and fluid nature of linear time. Timelines flow forward out of the "now" moment into the future, but they are being influenced continually by choices being made. Some of these choices may cause the timelines to shift, or even cease to exist. Other choices may bring new timelines into existence, so that apparently certain outcomes begin to fade, and new outcomes start to emerge. And all this moves and shifts and changes in a fluid way, more like the organic development of a life-form than the rigid mechanical working of a machine. This is what

47

makes any form of prediction so difficult.

Having said this, it is true that certain tendencies in the timelines can be followed, and from their development some idea of the shape of future events can be gained. But here we are entering the realm of multiple possible futures rather than the one future that your culture has conditioned you to expect. From these many possible futures, only a bundle of likely outcomes can be deduced, not a single outcome.

13

Overview of the Creative Process

Alariel: We are now nearing the end of the first section of these dialogues on how reality is created. As we have seen, Personal Reality Creation brings together energies from the Basic Mechanism and the Limiting Protocols in a process of great subtlety and complexity, yet the Basic Mechanism itself can be summarized quite simply:

> From within your bubble of experience,
> your consciousness sends a signal
> out into the Universe,
> which amplifies it
> and constructs a reality
> aligned with it.

When we add the operation of the Limiting Protocols, the tapestry of reality creation begins to weave a more complex pattern:

> The Limiting Protocols lift the operation
> of the Basic Mechanism
> out of the timeless realm of principles
> and into the focus of your time
> and your place
> by modifying the process
> through which your reality
> is created.

And through this interweaving there emerges an interplay of energies that underpins the whole process of human life and the way human beings manifest themselves upon the Earth:

> The general principles
> of the Basic Mechanism,
> combined with the constraints
> of the Limiting Protocols,
> shift reality creation
> from the universal to the personal,
> tailoring the process
> to your unique situation
> and your specific needs.

This combination of universal mechanism and personalized constraints is the result of a system of conscious choice. These constraints are chosen by your soul as a framework within which to learn and grow. Through learning and growing, you set aside the limitations that constrict the process of creating reality, and having transcended those limits, you move on to create reality upon other levels which are governed by different principles.

Having summarized Personal Reality Creation, it is now time to move on to consider these higher levels, and the principles involved in them. But already you can see how far Western culture has traveled in understanding these things. Compare, for example, the consciousness of a modern person living in the West with an inhabitant of ancient Greece. The Greeks perceived Divine Beings as all-powerful, and they saw themselves as frail and limited mortals who had to fit into the reality which the gods were creating.

The average person in your modern world now perceives life very differently, and they are able to take responsibility for their lives in a way that the ancient Greeks would never have been able to understand. Your spiritual journey in the West has reached a point where you can examine all the factors involved in creating your reality, and as the veil of forgetting dissolves, you are able, for the first time, to see this process clearly.

Through this knowledge you begin to see yourselves as you really are, and start to enter your own empowerment. Your world has come full circle since ancient Greece, and as your consciousness unfolds, you can see the truth which has been hidden for so long:

> YOU are the Creator-Beings,
> designing and manifesting
> whatever reality you wish.

Part Three:

The Bigger Picture

14

Three Key Relationships

Joanna: What do you think has been the biggest obstacle preventing us from understanding reality creation?

Alariel: What has set back the human understanding of reality creation more than anything else is the tendency to see it as a single process, a process that is isolated from all other processes. Personal reality creation does not stand alone, and it can only be fully understood as part of a greater whole, a bigger continuum of relationships that give it depth and meaning. Within this continuum, three key relationships need to be considered:

Relationship 1: The relationship of personal reality creation to the whole of reality creation.

Relationship 2: The relationship of the human personality to the whole human being.

Relationship 3: The relationship of personal reality creation to the timeframe of human spiritual development.

We will consider each of these relationships in turn.

Relationship 1: The relationship of personal reality creation to the whole of reality creation.

We perceive reality creation as having three main aspects:

1. Personal Reality Creation
2. Co-Creation
3. Instantaneous Creation

Although a complete understanding of these aspects of reality creation, their developmental interconnection and their potential, will be beyond the capacity of many human beings to grasp at this time, it is important to give the full range in outline here so that the vastness and diversity of the creative process can be understood.

We can summarize each of these aspects as follows:

Personal Reality Creation is the process that you have been experiencing on Earth for centuries now — it represents your past and your present.

Co-Creation is the destiny that is beginning to unfold for you — it represents your immediate future.

Instantaneous Creation is the supreme stage of reality creation — it represents your ultimate future as limitless Beings of Light.

We have already discussed Personal Reality Creation in some detail, and we will move on to consider Co-Creation and Instantaneous Creation in the next part of these dialogues.

Relationship 2: The relationship of the human personality to the whole human being.

A human being is rooted in the One Essence of the monad (also called the higher self) and manifests through the threefold soul (made up of higher mind, intuition and spiritual will) and down into a threefold personality (of physical body, emotional body and lower mind).

From this it becomes clear that a human being is a single, integrated organism, but also threefold (focusing through Body, Mind and Spirit) and sevenfold (a triple soul, a triple personality and a single monad).

Comment by Stuart: This analysis becomes much clearer when we see it in the form of a tabulation. I have added a column to reflect the function at each level:

Aspect	Level	Function
Higher Self	1. Spirit	Being
Soul	2. Spiritual Will	Purpose
	3. Intuition	Knowing
	4. Higher Mind	Understanding
Personality	5. Lower Mind	Thinking
	6. Emotional Body	Feeling
	7. Physical Body	Action

The session with Alariel continues:

Alariel: Our group has been monitoring the terms used to describe these levels, and recently we noticed a significant change. Twenty years ago the highest level was often called "the I AM Presence," but now there is a growing tendency to call this level "the higher self." Although "higher self" has been used in several ways in the past, this trend seems likely to become the norm and we have decided to follow it.

Relationship 3: The relationship of personal reality creation to the timeframe of human spiritual development.

As you move through the 2012 experience, you will be challenged to let go of all perceptions based upon duality and separation so that you can fully enter Oneness — a theme that we will return to later on. You will also be challenged to move from one form of reality creation to another form that is more in alignment with your pattern of spiritual development, and we will explore that under the heading of "Co-Creation."

When you begin to see personal reality creation within this greater framework, this structure of relationships, you begin to understand its real place in the scheme of things, and start to glimpse the arc of development underlying the whole system.

15

The Seven Steps
of Co-Creation

Joanna: You have mentioned the timing of reality creation. Could you please tell us what impact 2012 will have on all of this?
Alariel: Up to 2012 most human beings will be operating within the framework of Personal Reality Creation. As humanity moves through the 2012 experience, there will be a shift in focus away from this form of creation and towards Co-Creation.

Almost all of personal reality creation is karmic to some degree because absolutely pure and unselfish motivation is rare at the personality level. However, when you move on to a process of Co-Creation, you begin to leave karma behind. Here you will be creating from the soul level, rather than from the personality.

Do not expect this transformation to be instantly complete for every single human being when the moment of Transition comes. You have been operating at the ego level for thousands of years, and have got quite used to the feeling of personal reality creation, even if you have not understood the Principles which govern it. Transcending the ego level, focusing at the soul level, and settling into a process of Co-Creation will all take time to accomplish, yet after Transition, this will be the general direction in which humanity is traveling. There will always be eager pioneers surging ahead, and slow learners lagging behind, so regard it as a continuing process of change rather than an instant shift from one framework to another.

The Seven Principles of Being will apply as long as people continue to create their own reality at the personality level, and karma will still operate in the usual way at that level. It is only through entering a process of Co-Creation which focuses on the soul level that you begin to leave the whole machinery of karma behind.

Within the process of Co-Creation there are Seven quite distinct Steps:

1. Remember you are Spirit, you are Light.

This is about reconnecting with who you are, an essential first step because the creative process flows out from the core of your being. When you re-attune to your essential core, and affirm your oneness with the Spirit, many things become possible for you which you could never do from a focus at the personality level.

2. Hold the problem in the Light.

The process of Co-Creation solves problems and brings the solutions powerfully into manifestation. But first you need to focus on the problem and hold it in the Light. Just BE with the problem and allow it to be as it is. Hold it lightly and gently and just let it sit for a while in your mind.

3. Let the solution emerge and focus on it.

As you allow the problem to be as it is, the solution will arise automatically. Once you can see the solution, bring it strongly and clearly into the focus of your consciousness, so that you can retain it, and it will not drift away or shift into another form.

4. Within the stillness, let your faith increase.

Activity arises out of stillness. The greater the activity, the greater must be the stillness sustaining it. Sleep is stillness (although a very basic form of it) and centering, meditation and contemplation are more advanced forms of stillness. You need to have a strong and clear conviction that the solution you wish to manifest, will manifest. Your faith in the process working adds a vital link in the chain, and if your faith wavers or dissolves, Co-Creation will not occur. Do whatever is necessary to build up your faith: meditate, pray, chant, tone or use any other technique that works for you.

5. Affirm that it shall be so.

From the position of clarity and strong faith, send out an affirmation into the Universe that:

"It shall be so!"

This is trusting the Universe to do its part in the process of manifestation, and it clears the way ready for your most active phase in the process.

6. Do whatever is necessary.

Seek out whatever needs to be done to bring the solution into manifest reality, and do this yourself, or encourage others to share in this project if it is more than one person can achieve. Know that the Universe is doing its part, but is counting on you to do yours. This is where you "walk your talk" and demonstrate to others (and to yourself) that you are totally committed to this project. When all this is done, release the project into the care of the Universe, and get on with your life. Resist the temptation to keep worrying around the edges of the project, like an anxious sheep-dog. This is a sign that your faith in the Universe is not strong enough. If you feel a strong urge to do this, return to Step 4 and replenish your faith.

7. Give thanks.

This is where you complete the cycle, and give thanks to the Universe for loving and supporting you, and making this project possible. This is the final offering in the whole ceremony of manifestation.

Co-Creation helps to spread an understanding of the power of the Light. And the Universal Laws, like the Laws of Three and Seven, apply throughout the whole system. The process of Co-Creation may seem to be strongly sevenfold, but look a little closer and you will see that the Law of Three is at work here too:

Steps 1-3: Focusing the Light.
Steps 4-6: Grounding the Light.
Step 7: Completing the energy cycle.

So to summarize the Seven Steps of Co-Creation:

1   Remember you are Spirit, you are Light.
2   Hold the problem in the Light.
3   Let the solution emerge and focus on it.

4   Within the stillness, let your faith increase.
5   Affirm that it shall be so.
6   Do whatever is necessary.

7   Give thanks.

Of course it is perfectly possible to Co-Create before 2012, although many of your neighbors may not understand what you're trying to do, especially if they are deeply into the ego-dominated stage of their development.

Frankly, you've got a long way to go before the average man in the street grasps the principles of Co-Creation, or even sees any need for it at all. If anyone is happy working from the ego level, and is creating reality on that basis, any other approach will seem like "pie in the sky" to them.

And do not imagine that Co-Creation is entirely new, like something that will spring into existence for the first time around 2012. In fact, Co-Creation has been practiced on Earth for centuries, but only by advanced Beings like the Master-souls of humanity. Jeshua practiced it, as did all the great prophets before him, and shamanic teachers have practiced it throughout the ages. Until now, it has been very much a rarity, but with the Transition, all that will change. Co-Creation will soon become the way forward, the real future, for all humanity. And it will change from a minority interest to a mainstream concern.

The distance between Personal Reality Creation and Co-Creation is the journey from a life dominated by the personality to one illumined by the soul. It can be as long — or as short — a journey as you wish, depending upon the amount of resistance at the personality level. A great landmark upon this journey is the 2012 experience, when all the cosmic energies focusing upon this planet will encourage human beings to go through their own transition, in parallel with the Transition of the Earth. This landmark, this gateway into a better future for humanity, is an opportunity to move into the creation of a much better reality, a reality that is truly sustainable and will not exploit others or damage your planetary environment.

16

Instantaneous Creation

Alariel: We perceive the Cosmos as a Universal Web of Being which is made up of three components. Consciousness, Energy, and Matter. And although we refer to these separately, we know that they are not really three things, but different frequencies of one unified Existence. It is necessary to understand that in creating the Universe, Father-Mother God descends in vibrational frequency down from Light, down from pure formless Spirit to become the Universe. And in the process of God becoming the Universe, this Universal Web of Consciousness, Energy and Matter arises. This is the Supreme Grid into which all the other energy grids — cosmic, solar and planetary — fit.

The Creation of the Universe proceeds through an unfolding pattern of 1, 3 and 7 within a total environment of 12. The higher frequencies of Creation flow naturally towards 12, which is a summatory frequency, gathering together the lesser components within the greater whole.

Creation operates within a framework of Universal Law, the obvious examples being the Law of Three and the Law of Seven, since these numbers underlie the process through which Creation manifests. The manifestation process is overseen by the Elohim, who act as supervising Architects, consulting the Divine Plan which is the overall blueprint of Creation. And the specific designing and planning, and the shaping of form through Light, Sound and Vibration is undertaken by angels within the Host.

Within this framework of Universal Creation, we recognize a whole evolutionary cycle of Reality Creation by individual beings, beginning with Personal Reality Creation and moving through the stage of Co-Creation towards Instantaneous Creation, which is the ultimate process of manifestation. Instantaneous Creation occurs when there is an alignment of the individual with the Universal Web of Being.

The Universal Web contains linear space and time, but is not bound by these factors, for it also exists at the level of the Eternal Now. This Universal Web connects everything by being everything so that all levels, all places and all dimensions fit together in a vast Continuum. This holistic Web is all linked together, with an inter-signaling process connecting every level of each being horizontally (at that level) with all other beings, and vertically to integrate each individual. One of the results of this process of inter-connection is that space and time as you know it can be transcended, and information can be exchanged over vast distances. These exchanges involve a wide range of sentient beings including the humanity of planet Earth, and these beings are the focal point of the whole system of Universal Creation.

> You are the bridge between
> the inner and outer worlds,
> and the key connection between
> Consciousness, Energy and Matter.
> Your Consciousness directs the flow
> of Energy in the Universe,
> and the result is a series of realities
> created in Matter.

It is only at this comparatively late stage in these dialogues that the full outline of the process of reality creation can begin to emerge. The adding of the final element of Instantaneous Creation completes the picture so that the underlying threefold pattern can be recognized. If you look at the point of focus from which the creative process springs, this becomes clear:

Creative Process:	Focus of the Process:
Personal Reality Creation	The personality
Co-Creation	The soul
Instantaneous Creation	The Spirit (or higher self)

Whereas both the personality and the soul are bound (to differing degrees) by the limitations of linear space-time, the Spirit goes beyond those limits and creates instantly. In doing so, the Spirit transcends the laws of physics as you know them.

We do not regard linear time as the fourth dimension, seeing it instead as an aspect of the container which makes the physically manifested world possible, the framework which underpins the realm of form. From our perspective, each dimensional reality is a complete world of experience, inhabited by beings appropriate to that world. Thus, the third dimensional reality is host to physical human beings, the fourth dimensional reality (also known as the Interlife) is host to those who have died and are awaiting rebirth, and the fifth dimensional reality is host to ascended Beings. Linear time does not qualify as a world hosting sentient beings in this way, and that is why we put it into a separate category.

Feeling and belief are keys to the creative process at all levels. Creating comes from the heart, not from the head. At any of the three levels, you can use your focus to create a reality, but that focus is most effective when free of ego and judgment. Focus on the wish fulfilled, the outcome achieved, the reality created. In other words, focus on the experience of arrival at the destination and not upon the journey. Feel into and experience as fully as you can the answer, the solution, the achievement: don't lock yourself into the question, the problem, the journey. Enjoy the results rather than struggling with the process of achieving them.

This works at each of the three levels because by focusing in this way, you are aligning yourself with the Universal Web and the way the Web creates reality. Central to this creative process is a belief that this is really going to happen, but when that belief is strong enough to become faith, the whole process moves up a gear.

Through a faith-filled link with the Universal Web, you transcend time and create instantly. Faith is so important because it is the most intense and focused form that a core belief can take.

When you have complete faith your energy, from the higher self right down to the physical body, is aligned and focused in one direction. This is your whole being functioning in a state of Oneness. As Oneness is the nature of the Real, through the ability to function in this way, you resonate in harmony with the Universal Web, and can engage in direct and instant creation. From this it becomes clear that:

Instantaneous Creation is Oneness in action.

The key to Instantaneous Creation is reaching a level of faith so complete that you know the Universal Web will supply what is asked for. As a preliminary to reaching this point it can help to use the power of the imagination to create a picture of the end result of what you are asking for, but the real breakthrough happens at the level of faith. When the point of complete faith is reached, manifestation occurs instantly.

Some people will generate that level of faith by meditating, praying or chanting, but there are many other ways of approaching this. A few rare souls will simply pull the necessary faith out of their deep inner resources, but do not expect that to be possible for everyone. Most people will need to work at some kind of preparation process. Whatever method of preparation is used, when enough faith is generated, the Universal Web presents what is asked for in a way that transcends time.

In a state of complete faith, you not only believe that the manifestation will happen, you know it will happen. It is almost as if on some higher level of your being you have already seen it happen.

Through the exercise of complete faith, belief becomes knowing and knowing becomes manifestation. This is the ultimate sequence of reality creation:

I believe,
I know,
I manifest.

We move here into a high and subtle realm of consciousness, which so far has been explored by only the bravest of your spiritual pioneers, the Master-souls of humanity. But what they have discovered now stands ready to empower and liberate everyone, for the Earth is moving into Light, and your time has come. You are being challenged to go beyond your limitations and embrace your own empowerment. In doing so, be aware of entering a new realm of experience with its own logic:

When the Oneness in the individual
mirrors the Oneness of the Universe,
time and space are transcended
and anything is possible.

Here the knower and the known
come together in the Oneness of the Eternal Now.
Here limitations are forgotten
and you fulfill your destiny
as powerful Creator-Beings,
the Children of the Light.

Within this higher frequency of knowledge, clarity can be accessed on the whole arc of reality creation:

Focus:	Type of Manifestation:	Objective:
1. Personality	Personal Reality Creation	Personal expression
2. Soul	Co-Creation	Highest good of all concerned
3. Spirit	Instantaneous Creation	Oneness

The entire creative scheme is linked together so that resonances between levels illumine the whole process. Thus, even in the operation of core beliefs at the level of Personal Reality Creation you can see the greater process at work. A core belief is powerful because it starts to align your consciousness, giving you a single direction and a cohesive focus. The strongest form of core belief is faith, and complete faith brings into alignment all three aspects of a human being — personality, soul and Spirit. When a human being moves in an integrated and aligned way, they do not just use the creative process, they become that process. When creator and creation merge during manifestation, the energy of Oneness automatically transcends the duality of time and space.

This transcendent state of Oneness highlights the limitation and dysfunctionality of all other states of being. In comparison with this Oneness, it now becomes clear that manifestation at a lesser level is held into a sequence of time by the non-alignment of consciousness. When the consciousness moves into alignment, the locks holding the process into time dissolve, and the manifestation becomes instantaneous.

Hence, Instantaneous Creation should not be considered as a strange or unusual process. The unusual aspect of reality creation is the locking of your process into time through the non-alignment of consciousness. This is — from our perspective — a strange and laborious diversion away from the natural easy flow of energy which creates instantly when a consciousness is aligned. This experience of flow is the natural order of things, and this is the goal towards which you are moving through your emerging understanding of reality creation, and your awakening to your full potential as realized beings.

Part Four:

A Time of Change

17

From Religion to Spirituality

Joanna: Could you put the current breakthrough in consciousness into some kind of context for us? How did this breakthrough come about, and what led up to it?

Alariel: No breakthrough occurs in a random fashion, without deep underlying causes. There are always seeds planted before the time of rapid progress, and a point at which the new ideas seem to germinate in many minds around the same time. If you look at the pattern of human development, there are a whole series of breakthroughs followed by periods of consolidation when the new ideas are absorbed and worked out in practical ways. The times of breakthrough tend to begin in the 75th year of each century, with the period of consolidation focusing on the middle years of the following century. By the time you reach the year 75 again, humanity is usually ready for another breakthrough.

In the case of the consciousness revolution, all this began with Blavatsky in the 1870s, when she was working on her first major book, *Isis Unveiled*. This, together with *The Secret Doctrine*, laid the first foundation for all the expansion of consciousness that was to follow over the next century. Blavatsky's work popularized the Eastern ideas of reincarnation, karma and the existence of Master-souls, and firmly established these concepts within Western culture. It is not that the West was entirely ignorant of these ideas up to that point, but until Blavatsky came along, they were considered so uniquely oriental that they could safely be ignored. After she focused attention upon these concepts, they were put firmly on the intellectual agenda of the West.

Where Blavatsky led, others followed. The work of Rudolf Steiner, Alice Bailey and others consolidated that legacy, and extended the base of esoteric knowledge to include concepts such as rays, vibrations, the auric field, and energy-centers and energy-lines in the physical body. Without this essential information, the whole raft of new age therapies would have had no intellectual foundation.

In 1875, when Blavatsky was establishing this esoteric movement in the West, religion was still a powerful force — some would say one of the dominant forces in Western culture.

By 1975, when Seth's channeling on personal reality, and *A Course in Miracles*, and the Hurtak text on the keys of consciousness were going out into the world, that world had changed beyond recognition. Now it was Spirituality that formed the main impulse driving forward the agenda of the soul. The freedom to define God in line with one's own perception was beginning to develop into the ability of each individual to pioneer their own pathway to the Light.

A number of Churches reacted to the rise of Spirituality by funding research projects designed to prove that the New Age had a coherent theme and a single, integrated belief system. However, despite much effort, no convincing evidence could be found to back up these assertions. Since New Agers believe in a whole range of things, not just one thing, the theory that the New Age Movement was a cult did not stand up to close examination. The Churches, looking for a church-like organization capable of founding a new religion, discovered that there was no New Age credo, New Age Vatican or New Age bible. Instead of these things, they found a web of connections, a supportive global network linking kindred spirits, each following their own chosen path to the Light.

The path of individual autonomous Spirituality that was emerging was very different from an organized religion, and it needed none of the trappings of a Church to sustain it. It flowed on like a great river, with the wisdom of many traditions connecting with it and nourishing it. The sense of freedom and empowerment felt within this new Spirituality — a feeling of happy escape from doctrine and hierarchy — was an experience shared by many.

In other areas, there were similar stirrings towards freedom and autonomy. At the political level, the old dictatorships were starting to crumble, and social changes were readjusting the balance between men and women. At the same time, there was a realignment of perception within the sciences that was beginning to bring science and Spirit closer together. The combination of all these developments was generating a fresh energy and optimism, and in the midst of this ferment of change, the stage was set at last for a new beginning: the emergence of a New World and a New Consciousness.

Comment by Stuart: Alariel's focus on the 75th year of each century is interesting, and the dates of publication provide some confirmation of this point:

Title	Author	Publication date
Isis Unveiled	Blavatsky	1877
The Keys of Enoch	J.J. Hurtak	1973
The Nature of Personal Reality	Seth (channeled by Jane Roberts)	1974
A Course in Miracles	Channeled by Helen Schucman	1975

18

Personal and Planetary Changes

We already had some information on 2012, but felt we were only scratching the surface on this subject. Fortunately, during a session when our friend Cathie Welchman was present, we had the chance to explore this further with Alariel.

Cathie: What is the real significance of the year 2012?
Alariel: That year is like a window of opportunity.
Cathie: For what?
Alariel: For your planet to go into Transition and rise in consciousness and vibration. This process fits within the framework of an ascending and transforming Universe. The exact date of Transition will be decided by Gaia — the consciousness of the Earth — so take 2012 only as a guideline, and don't become obsessed with any particular date. A shift of this kind is a very special time, when the Light gets lighter, but the dark also gets darker and chaos spreads faster.

Joanna: How can human beings help in this process of Transition?
Alariel: You are being challenged to let go of all the heaviness in your lives and move onwards into Light. That is why you are raking over your past history so intensely at the moment: it needs to be accepted, forgiven and released. The old, rigid structures in your society need to dissolve and be replaced by lighter forms that honor the potential within all human beings.

All the elements in your life, including your thoughts, emotions and diet, need to move up into higher frequencies as a prelude to merging with your Light Body. It is the Light Body which will enable you to move effectively through the process of transformation.

Joanna: What does the Transition of the Earth mean for us in practical terms?

Alariel: When a planet begins to prepare for Transition, that focuses a vast amount of Light, which triggers off encoded keys in your DNA. This sends you a big "wake-up" call, and intensifies your energy field. That in turn affects your etheric body and stimulates every cell within your being to vibrate faster. It is affecting all your physical systems as they try to adapt to the higher frequencies, and from time to time, it may send your nervous and glandular systems into overload. The nervous system is being realigned and the glands are being restructured. And all this is leading to a great acceleration of consciousness.

It's going to be challenging from time to time, and may cause physical discomfort, disorientation — even minor illnesses. Headache, muscle pain, memory loss, and changes in sleep and eating patterns are all part of this same process. You may become anxious and irritable and unable to concentrate. And you may feel much more tired than usual. When that happens, relax, rest and honor the changes that are taking place. You are transforming faster than any previous generation, and should give yourselves credit for going through massive changes in such a short period of time.

The reason that the nervous system is being realigned and the glandular system is being restructured is because all this is necessary if you are to experience higher frequencies of consciousness. You simply would not have been able to handle the subtle frequencies that are now becoming accessible to you with your existing nervous and glandular systems. Do not underestimate the extent of the changes reaching right down to the physical level, and don't push yourself when you reach points of overload.

Try to regard it as an enormous opportunity. Frequencies of consciousness are now available to you that were not available before. When you look back and see the sort of beings that your grandparents were and you compare their vibration rate and consciousness with your present situation, the difference is clear. So many things are becoming possible for you that were simply not available to earlier generations, and would not be understood by them.

The really big change will be your shift from a limited third dimensional (or 3D) awareness into full fifth dimensional (or 5D) consciousness. When you look back to the consciousness you had before from the perspective of 5D consciousness, that earlier state of awareness will seem very crude and simplistic. Many of your present values are not even adapted to the logic of your 3D situation. For example, you encourage everyone on your planet to work for, and enjoy, a high standard of living, but if all the inhabitants of your planet tried to enjoy high living standards your planetary resources could not sustain that.

Yes, some of your leading thinkers and teachers are beginning to advocate "living lightly on the Earth," but this is actually a very old idea. The Native Americans were trying to do this — and being very successful at it — long before science and technology began to pollute and despoil the Earth. Even if 2012 was not arriving to transform the way you think, feel and live, you could not pursue your present path for much longer without turning parts of the Earth into a wasteland.

It's just as well then, that Gaia is setting the pace now, and through the process of Transition, is about to save you from yourselves.

Joanna: And will we get help and support from other realms of being as we go through these changes?

Alariel: Most definitely yes. If you are in contact with personal guides, they will be very active at this time, and the whole angelic realm stands ready to help in any way you find appropriate: all you have to do is ask!

Then there are Star Masters from a whole range of civilizations within your galaxy, especially Sirius, the Pleiades, Arcturus, Orion and Vega. And Star Masters from the galaxy of Andromeda will become increasingly important as you focus more and more on Oneness: they are the supreme teachers of Unity Consciousness, and how it can be applied in practical ways. Help is also available through the Ashtar Command: this brings together Star Beings from many civilizations focusing a wide range of multidimensional knowledge and experience.

So help is available now from the angelic realm, Star Beings within your own galaxy, and from the Andromedans who come from a different galaxy. This assistance, combined with ongoing help from your guides and human Master-souls, provides a complete structure of help and support as you go through this challenging time of rapid transformation.

Comment by Stuart: Our friend Sue Fraser has produced a helpful booklet called The Rays and Extraterrestrial or Star Masters: this is available through her website:

www.intuitionandrays.co.uk.

The session with Alariel continues:

Joanna: It's good to know that we'll be getting a lot of help. We certainly could not go on much longer in the old ways, and the Earth is already in crisis.

Alariel: As a species, you went well down the road towards creating an unsustainable reality for yourselves and for the planet which nurtures you. However, fortunately for you, there are Limiting Protocols for species as well as individuals! And that is why the species equivalent of Soul Override will ensure that you destroy neither your planet nor — through the misuse of nuclear technology — a good part of the solar system around you. In your selfishness as a species, you forgot that everything in the Universe is connected. That confers many advantages, but it also implies that there are limits on the amount of destruction that can be tolerated within the solar system and the galaxy beyond it.

What you are beginning to see here is the reality created by humanity as a species being limited and confined. In that respect, you are now at the very beginning of your understanding of how far the Limiting Protocols really extend. When the rules governing personal reality creation are much better understood on your world, it will be time to reveal the Limiting Protocols governing planets, solar systems and galaxies!

19

The Evolution of Channeling

Joanna: Could you give us a practical example of how consciousness has evolved over the last century?
Alariel: Yes. I think the channeling process would be a good example to take here.

There has been a lot of confusion over the channeling process, so we'll begin with a brief outline of the techniques involved. The longest established form of channeling is deep trance mediumship, a technique that has a long history in shamanic culture. This was the technique used by the seers and oracles of the ancient world, and more recently by Spiritualist mediums. When using this method, the channel is usually not aware of the information being channeled.

Then there are two forms of conscious channeling where the channel is aware of the information being received: there is a light trance process and also a full awareness process that does not involve a trance state. The main focus of these three techniques differs. Deep trance mediumship channeling is mainly focused on the spirits of the dead, although there are exceptional mediums who attract more advanced ascended sources. Light trance channeling and full awareness conscious channeling both focus on non-physical entities. This category covers a wide range of sources including ascended Masters, advanced Star-Beings and Angelic Beings.

Comment by Stuart: A tabulation may make this clearer:

Type of channeling:	Main focus:
1. Deep trance mediumship channeling	Spirits of the dead
2. Light trance conscious channeling	Non-physical entities
3. Full awareness conscious channeling	Non-physical entities

My own process is full awareness conscious channeling. It is like stepping to one side so that another aspect of consciousness can focus through me. I could also describe it by thinking of my consciousness as a stage. Normally my personality takes center stage, but when I want to channel I mentally step into the wings so that the channeling source — Alariel in this case — can take center stage and transmit whatever needs to be communicated. I remain fully aware as the observer of this communication process, and focus on locking on to the energy of the channeling source so that the stream of ideas can flow through me in a light and natural way.

The session with Alariel continues:

Alariel: There has been a complete evolution in channeling over the last hundred years. In the first few decades of the twentieth century, almost all the channeling was deep trance mediumship channeling. One or two conscious channels were working at that time, but they were rare indeed, whereas the Spiritualist movement was training more and more trance mediums. The situation today is quite different: conscious channelers are everywhere and although there are still a number of deep trance mediums, those of high caliber are comparatively rare.

This is partly the result of the current stage of development of humanity as a whole. When preparing for transformation and ascension, you need to maximize your focus at a conscious level, and pull all your powers into the present moment. So any process that takes you away from being here, now is a diversion from the main effort from the point of view of your spiritual development. The truth is that conscious channeling — especially full awareness conscious channeling — is more focused on being present than trance channeling, and so more in line with your current stage of development.

When channeling was being attempted in the early years of the twentieth century, human consciousness had not, with a few exceptions, advanced sufficiently to make conscious channeling a viable option. The difficulty of taking the ego-dominated personality out of the picture so that a clear enough stream of information could be accessed was just so severe at this point that the trance process was, for most people, the only way to get reliable and consistent channeling.

Deep trance is a very effective method (if practiced by a trained medium), but it is an artificial way of getting round the intrusion of the personality. It's artificial in the sense that a deep trance channel is locked into a state of consciousness that isolates them from the direct influence of the personality. Trance puts the personality "on hold" as it were, or as much "on hold" as the medium can manage. This locking into a state of consciousness is associated with changes in the way the body deals with consciousness-input, and it involves changes in the normal functioning of the body-mind link. The consciousness is artificially locked into a specific consciousness-gear for the duration of a deep trance channeling process — a gear that inhibits the normal functioning of the whole human being in an integrated energy-life mode. The focus of the medium's awareness is artificially narrowed down and held down in this way, so that they can do this work.

Because deep trance channeling is essentially so artificial a process, it has major drawbacks. Special conditions are required: a quiet room with subdued lighting and the oversight of a person who will be responsible for the safety of the medium. The medium should not be touched during deep trance, nor should they be brought back too quickly out of that process. Unexpected physical contact during trance can result in trauma and even long-term health problems.

Contrast this with the process of full awareness conscious channeling. The conscious channel knows what is happening all the time, and can return instantly to present awareness and the ability to interact with anyone in the room. It is a more natural, fluent and easy process compared to deep trance channeling, and conscious channels do not require a darkened room.

Joanna: How much of the channel's consciousness does the channeling source use during the channeling process?
Alariel: More than is generally recognized. There are three areas involved here:

First, the channeling source will use the language habitually employed by the channel, usually their native tongue, but if they grew up using a language of limited vocabulary and then adopted a mainstream language with a larger vocabulary, then the mainstream language would be chosen. The language chosen does influence the communications quite substantially. For example, Sanskrit has twelve words to describe consciousness, whereas English has only two: "consciousness" and "awareness." However, English does have many parallel words in other areas enabling subtle differences in meaning to be conveyed.

Secondly, the channeling source has to work within the vocabulary of the channel : if that vocabulary is large, the range of options in expressing ideas will be large, too.

Thirdly, the channeling source uses the concept-structure of the channel: someone trained as a scientist, for example, will have a different concept-structure to a person trained in some other field.

The combination of language-choice, vocabulary and concept-structure gives any communication a certain quality, pushing it in this direction or that. The degree that it is influenced away from the original idea-pattern of the channeling source is the distance from a perfect communication, but frankly we do not look for perfection within any channeling process. We have found that excessive aspiration towards perfection can bring its own problems.

Joanna: That is not very clear. Could you please explain why it should be so?

Alariel: Many human beings treat channeling as if it was a pronouncement from an omniscient source, whereas actually no such source exists at the individual level. We work regularly with Angelic Beings up to the level of Archangel, and the Archangels tell us that even the Elohim — the highest level of individualized Being in the Universe — do not claim to be omniscient. In planetary systems where there is free will, there are always unexpected outcomes, and that alone makes omniscience impossible.

However, we do understand the cause of this human tendency. Many human beings have been desperate to give away their power in order to stay as dependent children forever and not move on to being spiritual adults. In this situation, omniscience would be very useful indeed: you could lean upon it and never have to make up your own mind. However, the Universe will not support this pattern. Sooner or later, everyone is challenged to step forward in the light of their own consciousness and accept their own empowerment as spiritual adults.

Although individual channelers may approach channeling in a number of ways, there is still much common ground between them. For example, many conscious channels find that it is like being an interpreter. As the stream of ideas emerges, the channel clothes them with appropriate words. In a deep trance process, the source has more control over the vocabulary, which is one reason why some channelers have preferred this method.

Joanna: Some people say that a trance process is more accurate.
Alariel: It can be, but it depends on which trance medium is involved. An efficiently trained and highly evolved medium who is able to detach entirely from the influence of the ego would be capable of very accurately rendering the material, but we have to tell you that such mediums are very rare indeed. In most cases, there is some ego-attachment and that can result in an overlay of influence in communications received during a deep trance process. We realize this will not be a popular idea to put forward because a number of people have cherished the illusion that any deep trance process is a guarantee of complete clarity and integrity of the material channeled.

However the human ego is a great deal more tenacious and devious than most people imagine, and influencing deep trance communications is quite within its capacity if the medium's psyche is at all flawed in an ego direction. This does not mean that the medium is trying to deceive, but they simply do not know their own consciousness well enough to be aware of their limitations.

Comment by Stuart: I can provide an illustration of this from my own experience. My mother, Beatrice Wilson, was trained as a deep trance medium by Grace Cooke, the White Eagle medium, in London in the 1930s. Bea was a very high-minded and sincere person, but I noticed when I was a child and observed her seances that there was a flaw in her channeling process. She could bring through much interesting and useful information, but any communications concerning the beautiful houses we were soon to move into were always suspect. None of this information was accurate, and the predictions in this area never came true. I concluded that this information on beautiful houses was just the result of wishful thinking on my mother's part, and these desires and aspirations had somehow got entangled with her messages.

The session with Alariel continues:

Joanna: So you regard deep trance as a flawed process?
Alariel: Please do not think we are being unduly negative or critical of trance channeling. In its day, it was the main channeling technique on your planet, and it has produced remarkable communications that have guided and will continue to guide humanity towards the Light. But it is simply that we take a broad view in observing the overall pattern of human spiritual growth, and from that perspective, the main emphasis has now moved on to conscious channeling. The few outstanding deep trance mediums that remain continue to serve magnificently in this way, but they are now isolated examples of a technique perfected in an earlier stage of your development.

Perhaps taking two examples, one from each type of channeling, will show you what we mean by this. Let us take a typical channel in each case.

The typical deep trance medium of the 1930s would channel in a very grounded way, fully embodying the energy of the guide (and it usually was a guide) so that the observer could get a sense of the whole physical presence of the channeling source. This meant that the delivery would be slow and deliberate, with the choice over words being dictated by the channeling source. The seance would take place in a darkened room, with one small light source, often a candle, and the channel remained seated with eyes closed during the seance.

Contrast this with the typical conscious channel of today: the Master (and it usually is a human Master-soul, or an Angel or Star-Being of similar unfoldment) is channeled in a light way that can lead to rapid, fluent delivery covering a much wider range of consciousness and more subtle options. The channel controls the vocabulary, and the stream of ideas being translated into words comes faster, more easily and more fluently. The channel is usually seated with eyes closed, but normal lighting is quite acceptable.

This gives examples of typical middle-of-the-road exponents of each form of channeling, but the exceptional full awareness conscious channeler can go far beyond this level. When securely locked in to the energy of the channeling source, they can move fluently in and out of the channeling mode. They can be talking from the usual focus of their personality one moment and be channeling the next, and you'll never notice the switch. Their eyes stay open, they can look at you and engage with you and still manage to deliver rapid and fluent channeling. The very best conscious channelers can even do this during workshops. They can engage fully with their audience, and move fluently in and out of channeling mode so that channeling simply becomes a frequency of consciousness that they can access at will. Here you see the example of a consciousness operating simultaneously on three levels: the stream of channeling information, the awareness of being locked onto the channeling source, and an observer awareness coordinating the whole process and ranging beyond it to interface with the environment.

One can also give an example of conscious channeling being used in another context: a therapist can interact with their guides and helpers during a session with a client, and the client may never know that the therapist is channeling at all.

How different these advanced processes are from the 1930s scene in the darkened room!

Yet in saying this, we are not implying that you should undervalue trance channeling as a technique. Deep trance channeling has had a very long and distinguished history, stretching back into the earliest stages of the shamanic tradition. This is the method used by the Oracle of Delphi and the other major oracles and seers in the ancient world.

Deep trance channeling is now approaching the end of its developmental cycle, but the development of conscious channeling is only just beginning. That is the real comparison between these two processes, and the essential point we're trying to make.

The evolution of the channeling process is a good example of how human consciousness is moving forwards from slow, sometimes awkward and lumbering techniques, to methods that are essentially faster, lighter and more flexible. There's a whole arc of development here. Channeling in the 1870s was a serious, difficult and hazardous business, but it has developed a light, versatile and playful quality that shows you the direction that the whole consciousness of humanity is moving in.

Joanna: So how should we regard channeling to get the most out of it?
Alariel: In three main ways.

Firstly, as just a "second opinion," a different viewpoint to lay alongside your own perceptions.

Secondly, as an opportunity to expand your consciousness and explore new perspectives.

Thirdly, as a way of increasing the flow of information between soul and personality, making this link stronger and more effective.

Channeling can open up new horizons, new ways of looking at the world. It should be nourishing and empowering, and strengthen your capacity to obtain inner guidance. However, if anyone is using the channeling they receive from someone else as a complete replacement for their own inner guidance, they are misusing the process. Channeling was never intended for this purpose, and your own inner guidance should remain paramount.

You have been receiving channeling from a wide range of sources — human Master-souls, Star-Beings and Angels — but now a further stage in the evolution of channeling is beginning to open up for you. It will soon become important for you to channel the totality of your Being — or at least as much of that totality as you can manage. In practical terms, this means channeling the energy and quality of your soul, letting your soul speak through you and color all your perspectives of life. Through constant attunement in this way, you begin to live the life of the soul, even while you still have an active personality.

When the soul illumines the personality, the ego becomes confined to a function of individual-awareness (where it can still be useful), rather than having free range as the master of the personality (where it can cause chaos). And as that soul-influence becomes stronger, you will find yourself increasingly channeling the highest aspect of your total Being: the higher self.

Let us be clear about this. When you channel the energy and wisdom of your higher self, you will not need to channel any other Being or energy-source. Everything you need, and need to know, is accessible through the higher self, and channeling the higher self will eventually become the only form of channeling that is relevant to you. However, we say "eventually" because channeling the higher self is an advanced stage, indeed the ultimate stage of the whole channeling process.

20

The Crystal Children

Joanna: Did we get a lot of help from outside our planet to start establishing the consciousness revolution?

Alariel: Yes, a lot of help, and from a number of sources. There has been much behind-the-scenes help supplied by Star-Beings, not through dramatic UFO landings and first contact, but through suitable individual humans being given information through channeling and the overlighting of consciousness.

Meanwhile, a parallel process of active communication has been occurring from the angelic world, resulting in a plethora of angel books and images. After being relegated to a dusty back-room in the Western mind, a remnant of the days of religious domination, suddenly angels were back in fashion again. And the channeling of angelic beings, which was almost non-existent in the 1930s, suddenly became a major element in the whole channeling process.

But the most dramatic, and in some ways the most far-reaching help of all, is coming from the advanced children, many from distant star-systems, who are now being born on planet Earth. It's as if the other star civilizations are sending their brightest and their best souls to give you a helping hand as you struggle upwards toward the Light! This is a major new development for your planet, and I want to talk a little about these new children.

From about 1980 onwards, a new kind of child started to be born on this planet. You may already have heard about the

Indigo Children, who came to break down structure and start to move consciousness forward out of the set traditional patterns that had dominated human thinking. The Indigos are important, but they were only the first pioneers in a whole wave of New Children. The main focus has now moved on to the Crystal Children, so-called because of the quality of their auric field.

The Crystal Children are building on the foundations laid down by the Indigos. They are doing this by focusing humanity on the vital importance of Oneness, which is not only a key theme in the present stage of your development, but an expression of the fundamental Reality of the Universe. The pattern of human culture up to this point has focused on the differences between your traditions, and in a time of global communications and rapidly expanding technology, this line of development is now proving too dangerous for you to pursue. What is now needed is a fresh perspective, a new way of looking at your differences as complementary parts of a greater Whole. This is exactly what the work of the Crystal Children will provide.

We have already communicated a good deal of detailed information about the Crystal Children, and do not intend to repeat all this information here. We simply wish to signal at this point that the Crystal Children are important to the future development of humanity, and will play a key role in preparing you for the 2012 experience. They can only be effective in playing this role because the whole system of communications on your planet, and the technology associated with it, has developed rapidly and become much more flexible and global. The capacity of the internet to link like-minded people throughout the world is a great gift to progressive minorities who need to band together in the early stages of pioneering new ideas and new ways of living and being. For this reason, we regard the internet as an essential technology underpinning your consciousness revolution.

Although your language is changing and evolving in line with new communications needs, do not imagine that word-based communications will be the only expression of the new consciousness. Many of the Crystal Children are telepaths of remarkable ability: they can signal telepathically using words, but much of their subtler communications take the form of telepathic signaling using advanced geometrics. We are not talking here about fixed geometrical shapes, but fluid patterns and symbols which change and evolve as the "conversation" develops. The point about using advanced geometrics is that the Crystal Children can signal telepathically in this way at prodigious speed — much faster than any human being can talk.

This technique has the advantage of transcending the need for translation, and it can cover subtle areas of consciousness where words would be inadequate. When you leave the lower levels of the personality and enter the frequencies of the soul, much of the information is beyond word-based language, and beyond the limitations of the concrete mind. In these subtle levels of the higher mind and the intuition, pearlescent and iridescent colors, symbols and geometrics combine to make a language of their own. This is the universal communication medium of the soul, linking all human beings into a common heritage of collective understanding.

Comment by Stuart: Alariel has contributed a whole section on the New Children to our second book, *Power of the Magdalene*, published by Ozark Mountain Publishing (see Further Reading under 'Wilson.')

Some information on the New Children (including details of key books and websites) can be accessed by visiting our website, www.foundationforcrystalchildren.com. But for the moment, we can give here a brief extract on the structure of the New Children based on Alariel's communications to put them into some kind of perspective:

The full spectrum of the New Children comprises:

Indigo Children, born from about 1930 onwards but first arriving in large numbers in the 1970's. Indigos are intelligent, aware, sensitive, powerful and vibrating at a higher rate than the average child. They have a broad range of creative, healing and consciousness-related powers which develop naturally as they grow older.

Super-Psychic Children, born from about 1950 onwards. The Super-Psychics possess a wide range of psychic and paranormal powers including telekinesis. They are very challenging to anyone with a scientific training, and can transcend many of the established laws of physics.

Crystal Children, born from about 1980 onwards, with significant numbers coming in from 1990. Crystals are:
1   Powerful, but super-sensitive and empathic.
2   Highly intelligent, but often intuitive rather than academic.
3   Accepting and inclusive rather than judgmental.
4   More inclined to share than to compete.
5   Deeply into the practice of Oneness (or Unity Consciousness.)

Rainbow Children, born from about 2000 onwards. These are the inheritors of the whole build-up of these new energies. These wise and gentle beings represent creativity beyond ego, life beyond separation and achievement beyond struggle.

Part Five:

Awakening to the Real

21

The Three Realities

Joanna: Is our reality the only reality that exists?
Alariel: No. There are actually three realities of which your
    reality is only one:

1   The Unmanifest
2   The Greater Reality
3   The Lesser Reality.

    The Unmanifest is the level of Divine Being beyond the
manifested Universe. This is the "Great Mystery" of Native
American spiritual teachers, and the "Godhead beyond God"
of Meister Eckhart. In this unmanifest level, the blueprint of
the Divine Plan is upheld. This is the Cosmic Stillness from
which all creation flows.
    This Unmanifest level, which is also called the "Source"
and the "Void," is spaceless and timeless, and is beyond
human comprehension. This is the unmanifest seed from
which the manifest creations spring, creating time and space,
and into this Void, these creations will eventually dissolve,
when both time and space cease to be. The Void has no limits
— being limitless, timeless and spaceless, it simply IS.

    The everyday life you experience on planet Earth forms
the Lesser Reality and is essentially a third dimensional
experience. You live at the third dimensional (or 3D) level,
and have periods of rest, recuperation and reflection in the

Interlife at the fourth dimensional level (or 4D.) The 3D and 4D worlds form a closed loop of experience which has been described as the wheel of birth, death and rebirth. When you die, you enter 4D, but you have to ascend to enter the fifth dimensional reality (or 5D), and this level forms the beginning of the Greater Reality.

Joanna: When I was driving along, I was thinking about this whole thing. I realize from the spiritual point of view, this is all maya, all illusion, but I am in a human body having a human experience. This experience is very real to me, so at this point of time in my body, that does seem to be my reality.

Alariel: Yes, we would agree. We do not agree with those spiritual teachers who discount the present level that human beings are experiencing and say that it is so illusory that it does not exist. For you, it definitely does exist, and it seems to be a persuasive and tangible reality. It may not be the only reality out there, but that's another question. We think it is important to acknowledge and respect all the levels of creation, and this reality of yours is part of creation, and therefore, deserves respect.

What is illusory about it is that it seems to be the only reality, the total reality of the whole Universe. This is where the illusion lies, in your experience seeming to be all and everything, not in the fact of its existence.

So, despite what some teachers say, we continue to insist that the Lesser Reality does indeed exist, and as part of God's creation, it requires and demands respect. This is the source of our perspective, for we are determined that all aspects of God's creation, however imperfect they may be, shall still be accorded the respect they deserve.

Joanna: You say the Lesser Reality is imperfect, but surely a perfect God can only create a perfect creation.

Alariel: An interesting question. The Lesser Reality is indeed imperfect, for it is not aligned with the Truth of Oneness, but it is also perfectly adapted to your needs at the third dimensional level of experience. In the wisdom of God, sometimes even the imperfect can be perfect!

Joanna: And what makes a Reality — how can you distinguish it from another Reality?

Alariel: The definition of a reality is a world which cannot be seen by those possessing the ordinary sight of a lower dimension. Thus, for example, those who have died and are present in the fourth dimensional reality (which is the Interlife or the space between lives) will not be visible to anyone living in 3D who has the ordinary vision of that plane of existence. In the same way, fifth dimensional beings will not be visible to those in the Interlife who possess only normal 4D sight.

The Greater Reality consists of the fifth dimensional reality and all the other dimensions above that level.

Joanna: How many dimensions are there in the Greater Reality?

Alariel: We will not enumerate these dimensions, nor will we describe them at this point because we consider that would be a distraction from the task which now faces you. Humanity has quite enough to do to transcend the 3D paradigm with all its obsession with duality, and step into the non-dual existence of the fifth dimension. This will be quite challenging enough for you in the short term, and we therefore suggest that you focus upon it and do not concern yourselves too much with the dimensional realities that exist beyond 5D. All you need to know at this stage is that the Universe consists of a number of dimensional realities, which in time you will be able to explore.

The Greater Reality is founded on and reflects an essential Oneness, and the distance from the Lesser to the Greater

101

Reality is a moving towards, and merging with, that Oneness. Oneness will require a complete reorientation of your consciousness, and that will be a major shift for you.

Vengeance, for example, becomes absurd within a framework of Oneness. If only God exists, if all life is an interconnected Web of Being and Consciousness, then who exactly would you be taking revenge upon?

Your aim should now be to focus on the Oneness that you all share, rather than any small differences that may seem to divide you. When you focus on this Oneness, you will be challenged to stay in that Truth, whatever happens in your life. This is when the Universe will test you, and events will occur to plumb the depth of your commitment to the Truth. As soon as you start to edit and modify Oneness in your mind and say, "I can forgive anyone except So-and-so," then Oneness disappears.

You are challenged to include all beings in Oneness, even those you least like and respect. You can condemn their actions, their behavior — as Jeshua did with the money-changers in the Temple — but you should NOT condemn them as beings. In exactly the same way, you may not approve of the behavior of a very young child, but you can still love and include that child.

What Jeshua taught was a way of staying centered in Oneness. Forgiveness helps you do this, while non-forgiveness pulls you out of Oneness and into the energy of duality — the tug-of-war between you and this person you don't want to forgive. However much they may have hurt you, by refusing to forgive them, you are continuing with the energy of this hurt, and damaging yourself. Any deviation from the path of Oneness causes some damage to your inner life, and that damage should be repaired as soon as possible through the process of forgiveness.

Oneness may seem a gentle and comfortable idea to many people, but that is only because they have not fully understood its implications. Oneness as non-duality can be very tough and challenging indeed. Your world is constantly feeding you images of duality, and to ignore all this and focus on the essential Oneness of things is a difficult task. That is why it is so important to listen to the Crystal Children, for they are Masters of Oneness and can help you to escape from the dualities which have influenced your world for so long.

The dualistic paradigm has made it very easy for you to love your friends and hate your enemies. However, it has become so ingrained in human consciousness that it is distorting your perceptions, and making peace between warring neighbors on your planet very difficult to achieve. The challenge now facing humanity is to lay aside the divisive dualistic way of thinking and feeling, and start looking for common ground — the basis for friendship and co-operation.

22

The Way of Light

*Joanna: As your group has been working on a number of star
systems, have you seen other civilizations go through a
process similar to the Transition of the Earth?*

Alariel: Yes, we have. The cultural quality and technological
advancement of civilizations may vary, but they all follow a
broadly similar process of development. Although, it must be
said that no planet as densely physical as the Earth has ever
ascended, so far. Humanity wished to have a more intensely
physical experience than other civilizations — more ecstasy,
even if that also meant more agony. That drove your planet,
and the human consciousness linked to it, much further down
into matter than any other star system of which we are aware.

*Joanna: And are there any accounts of this process which might
help us as we go through our own Transition?*

Alariel: Yes. There are a number that are quite full of insight, but
many of these accounts only have real meaning within their
culture of origin. However, we have found some which are
more universal, and there is one in particular, from a
civilization in the galaxy of Andromeda, which you might
find helpful. This text is called "The Way of Light" and we
are happy to share it with you now:

All beings who experience the worlds of form
pass through three stages in their journey:
  Dreaming,
  Stirring,
  Awakening.

In Dreaming, the little me sees itself
as proudly separate,
and contained within its self-conceit
it prances wildly like a foolish child.

In Stirring, the little me
gets glimpses of a greater Self,
a larger picture and a higher Truth.
These glimpses, fleeting at first,
swell and gather till they bring
chaos and confusion to its crumbling world.

In Awakening, the little me
surrenders to the greater Self,
and through the realization of that Self
knows that it is One with all of life.
As the bubble of illusion fades,
the Eternal I rises like the Sun,
illumining the life
with Love and Power and Truth.

In the radiance of that Truth,
the manyness of forms is recognized
as misperception,
a distortion that exists
only in the dream-world of the little me.
It stands revealed as the Grand Illusion,
for in the higher realms of Light,
only the One exists.

Here the veil falls away,
and the true Essence is revealed:
with Oneness as the Source,
and the Reality of things.

And when the Self shines forth,
the Truth at last is clear:

One Energy and Consciousness in all that is,
and all existence as one Web of Life.

When this is understood,
the voyager is home at last,
all burdens lifted,
and all shadows gone.
For now the heart is whole once more,
and all its hurts are healed.

Joanna: Thank you for sharing this text with us, it is quite wonderful. We appreciate that the process of Transition will bring many changes into our lives. Could you give us some idea of how the guidelines for our development will evolve as we move through these changes?

Alariel: Certainly. This will all become much clearer as your consciousness begins to clarify and the veil fully dissolves. As you progress and expand your consciousness, the principles which guide your development will change and evolve to keep pace with this expansion.

We have spoken of the Seven Principles of Being which govern the process through which you manifest your reality at the third dimensional level, but there are a further three Higher Principles which guide your development at the fifth dimensional level and beyond.

As you are fast reaching the point where the veils are lifted and you awaken to who you really are, it is time for you to review the whole process of manifestation at the third dimensional level, and that is why this information is being given now.

At the end of every stage of development, there is the possibility of insight, the reaching of clear understanding of what has been involved in that stage. It is as if you review that cycle of development and see it clearly for the first time, and this reviewing process is part of the preparation for moving on to the next stage.

You are about to move through a time of Transition and enter a new stage of learning and growing, this time at the fifth dimensional level. Here, different rules apply because the individual begins to merge more and more into the Oneness which is your real nature.

As the veil falls away, the seductive lie of separation is revealed for what it is, and the Truth of Oneness shines forth within a consciousness illumined by these Higher Principles:

1   All Life is One,
and all consciousness shares
in one holistic state of being.
Although the functions and expressions
of that consciousness may vary,
in essence, Consciousness remains One,
and is not divided.

2   In the higher realms of Light,
only God exists,
and Beings of Light who resonate
with the nature of God,
which is Love and Light.

3   Ascending into the fifth dimensional Reality
is only the beginning of your journey
into the subtle realms of being.

Ahead of you there are many worlds
yet to be explored.

A new understanding of the nature of consciousness is beginning to flower within you, coupled with the development of a Language of Light which is still only at the fringes of your perception. You are leaving behind the stage of being a spiritual child, and reaching out towards the possibility of becoming an independent spiritual adult, fully awakened, fully unveiled, and standing in the Light of your own Consciousness.

Part Six:

New World,
New Consciousness

23

The Advancement of Consciousness

Alariel: One of the big problems on your planet is that many people think their consciousness is fixed at birth, and cannot change or grow. The evolution of form is now well established in your minds, but the evolution of consciousness is still considered a revolutionary idea.

The truth is that consciousness has evolution built into it at a very fundamental level. This is something that the New Children will soon be demonstrating to you, as Indigos develop into Crystal Children, and Crystals move on to become Rainbow Children. You don't live in a static Universe, so why should your consciousness be static? Change and growth are part of the very fabric of life, and should be embraced with enthusiasm.

The more you can see yourselves as a spectrum of consciousness and energy (expressed through a physical body but not bound by it), the more you'll be able to advance your consciousness and move forward along the path of your spiritual evolution. And the more you think of yourselves as multidimensional beings, the more you'll be able to experience and develop your multidimensional skills.

This is the kind of open-ended and progressive approach that we would like to encourage:

> I am a multidimensional spectrum
> of consciousness and energy,
> evolving within the Web
> of All That Is.

Part of that evolution is rediscovering the real meaning of play. The wise person watches their children and learns from them. The Hindus, who have a subtle and long-established spiritual tradition, say that "God plays." This concept helps you to respect and value play, and takes you away from an unhealthy obsession with work as the only worthwhile thing in life.

The whole 2012 experience is going to give the advancement of consciousness a big boost, so prepare for this to become a major talking point. Humanity has invested a vast amount of time in the advancement of science and technology: it's time the advancement of consciousness received your attention. This is where many of the exciting developments and breakthroughs will come during the present century. The time for focusing outwards is now drawing to a close: the new challenges are emerging in innerspace, not outer space. This is the new frontier, the area of optimum growth. The exploration now confronting you is the exploration of your own consciousness and its energy system, and how that consciousness and energy is connected to the consciousness and energy of the Universe.

You have made giant strides in your technology during the last hundred years, but the strides you will make in your consciousness will amaze you. Instead of moving slowly across your solar system strapped into giant rockets, you will be able to move instantly across the vast reaches of interstellar space. Instead of being merely citizens of your planet, you are now challenged to become Citizens of the Universe.

Step forward boldly into this new world of advancing consciousness and the development of multidimensional energy skills.

Go forward with confidence upon your journey of exploring all the possibilities of your own being.

Move forward joyfully in the knowledge that the angelic world stands ready to help and support you as you enter this new stage of your unfoldment.

But even this is not the end of your process of growth, and there is a stage beyond the advancement of consciousness. This is a stage of pure Being, where you're *there* already as a Child of the Light. Yes, you need to advance in consciousness and the skillful use of energy to reach that point of Being (or more exactly to *return* to it, because it's something you had before you descended into form.) But be prepared also for a stage at which all your advancing is done and you are content simply to BE.

24

Transition and the Big Questions

Joanna: Will the new consciousness divide people?

Alariel: The big divide is going to be between those who can grasp the outline of the Transition to some extent, and those who don't want to take on board any idea of change and wish to continue thinking in purely materialistic terms. Clinging to the old may cause the latter group much suffering during this period. For change will come, whether they are ready for it or not.

If one clings to the outer form, life seems full of loss and despair, and there is no comfort anywhere. But if one focuses on the life within the form, there is always the possibility of new hope and unexpected joy. This is a time for looking forward in expectation of all things being made new, and not a time to look back in sadness for what has been lost.

It is both a continuous arc of change and an opportunity from your point of view. There is now a swift route into the Light, a route enabling you to go through change in lighter and easier ways. The more you release the heaviness of your past, the more you can lighten up in your diet, your lifestyle choices, your vibration and your consciousness, the easier it will become to move on and enjoy the whole process. Even time will work for you and smooth your path if you embrace the lighter way of living, and you'll be able to skip through the last part of your chosen work in very little time indeed. You'll be amazed at how quickly and easily things can go forward because the Universe will support those willing to take the leap of faith and ascend vibrationally at this time.

Joanna: There is much confusion at present over exactly what ascension entails. Could you clarify this for us please?

Alariel: Yes. In ascension, you raise your whole being up into the higher-vibrational level of Light. There are two stages in ascension: an initial stage of spiritual ascension followed by a stage of full ascension. The distance in time between these two stages is determined by how long it takes you to finish your self-appointed task here on Earth, the mission which your soul has volunteered to carry out.

The whole ascension process is affected by the way humanity is linked together. Humanity is linked in three ways: genetically through the DNA, in consciousness through the Collective Unconscious, and vibrationally through the Collective Energy Field. The link through the Collective Energy Field enables you to be aware of what is happening to those close to you wherever they are. If, for example, someone loved by you dies many miles away, you will feel the shock of that event as an impulse of energy traveling through the Collective Energy Field.

All three parts of this system transmit and receive information, so it's really a vast integrated information system. The DNA transmits changes in DNA structure, the Collective Unconscious transmits changes in awareness, and the Collective Energy Field transmits changes in vibration.

All three are linked together so that changes in any one system affect the other two systems. Thus, as your consciousness changes, your DNA evolves and your vibrational level rises.

The vibrational level of the Collective Energy Field determines what happens to you when you reach the second stage of ascension. Two thousand years ago the vibrational level was so low that when a human being merged with the Light and ascended, he or she had to leave physical incarnation. At that time, they could not sustain a physical body after ascension because the difference in vibrational levels was too great. That is why the Essenes and other spiritual groups saw ascension as a going into Light and a stepping out of physical incarnation into a state of formless being.

While ascension two thousand years ago would inevitably have separated you from the physical world, ascension now gives you access to a more abundant life while STILL staying in a physical body on this planet. Thanks to the evolution in human consciousness, this new option has opened up for you:

You can now ascend and stay here
on this planet in a physical body.

Some human beings may continue to dissolve their physical bodies into Light and ascend in the traditional way, but this will only apply if the soul has chosen to serve in places other than the Earth. There are many places in which to serve in this Universe, but it is hoped that most humans will, when they reach ascension, choose to continue to serve upon the Earth and help to create the New World.

Comment by Stuart: What effect the Transition of the Earth will have on our consciousness is one of the Big Questions of our time. And it was Alariel's willingness to answer Big Questions which made our dialogues with him so rewarding. He was always very positive about the benefits of a questioning approach, and at one point he said:

"The Big Questions are useful because they stretch the mind and challenge you to go beyond what you already know. By doing that, they encourage you to consider new possibilities. A Big Question is like a door which opens onto a new perception of life, an invitation to go upon a journey of exploration."

A few of these Big Questions seem to be timeless. They hold an enduring fascination, and keep turning up in one form or another:

Where did we come from?
What is our real nature as human beings?
What should we be doing now?
What is the purpose of life?
Where are we going?

Alariel's answers to these Big Questions give a fascinating insight into his perception of humanity and the human condition. In one case, the answer comes not only from Alariel's whole group of angels, but from a much bigger research process involving both human beings and beings from other Star Civilizations.

Joanna: Where did we come from?
Alariel: You came from the Light, which is Spirit. You are Children of the Light. The Light is Consciousness, but it is also Energy. It can be formless, but projected downwards, it can crystallize into physical matter.

Joanna: What is our real nature as human beings?
Alariel: You have all the qualities and powers of the Light, and at its deepest level, the Light is Love. These two key aspects of Spirit — Light and Love — are your true nature, your real and essential Being. When you express Light and Love, you are being true to the Self within.

Joanna: What should we be doing now?
Alariel: Knowing that this question might come up in our dialogues at some point, I have consulted my colleagues within our angelic group, and together we have also researched the views of a number of human Master-souls and

117

advanced Star Beings. By consulting widely, we are able to draw upon a broad range of experience. Based on this research, we have drawn up a list which may provide a comprehensive answer to your question:

1. Focus on being here, now in a positive way. A great spiritual teacher once expressed this as loving where you are, what you are doing and who you are with. This is excellent advice and we could not improve upon it.

2. Don't be too obsessed with controlling your own process by trying to understand it. The pace of change is now becoming so fast that the logical mind will never manage to keep up. The more reliable feedback is from your intuition. It's much faster than the linear mind and will help you surf the wave of spiritual energy into 2012 and beyond.

3. Those wishing to go forward into accelerated development at this time will be given support in two main ways: through inner guidance as they progress along their spiritual path, and through teaching and methodology transmitted during sleepstate. For this, it is important to prepare each night by staying in a quiet contemplative state in the hour immediately before retiring.

4. Ignore the dinosaurs who are resisting change. They have no real relevance in your changing and evolving world. Don't give them energy by opposing them, just let them fade away.

5. Treat the whole of your life as an oracle system, which is giving you subtle hints and guidance. What is the Universe telling you about yourself? How is the pattern of your life mirroring your inner world?

6. Don't be drawn in to the drama of those around you, or into the events that are unfolding on the world stage. Faced with many warring dualities, you can still choose to stay in the transcendent peace of Oneness.

7. Be gentle with yourself, and nourish yourself as you go through the process of change. Remember that play is a great healer, and can lead to creative breakthroughs when you're in a relaxed and playful state. So give yourself time to unwind, rest, relax and play.

8. Express joy in your life. Sing, dance or do whatever makes you feel most joyful. Know that at the very core of your being you are Love, you are Light, you are Joy!

9. The heart has its own magic — listen to your heart and let it guide you. Visualize all beings within a circle of Love and say:
    Through the magic of the heart
    I hold all beings
    in the Circle of Love.
    May all beings be blessed
    and move towards the Light.

10. The key to creating a better reality is to maximize the application of your talents and minimize the impact of your limitations. It is through exploring those talents, transcending those limitations, and creating the reality you want, that you begin to understand your full potential as human beings.

Joanna: Thank you. Those are very practical steps. Can we ask one of the biggest questions now: What is the purpose of life?
Alariel: Life is about BEING. To BE in a formless state is limitless in one sense, since consciousness has no boundaries. You might remain upon the formless level and try to imagine

what a sunset over the mountains would look like, or how the wind would sound rustling the leaves in a great forest, or what effect the waves would have as they lap upon a beach in the warm sunlight, but only by BEING there in a physical form can you fully appreciate these things.

The purpose of life is to explore consciousness and energy — to experience life within form, and through transcending form to reach a deeper understanding of energy and consciousness.

Joanna: Where are we going?

Alariel: You are going to a state of expanded Being in which you are entirely Light. You came from the Light, and to Light you will return.

Joanna: But if it's a round trip, a circular journey back to our point of origin, what's the point of it all?

Alariel: You go out like an acorn and come back like an oak tree: both are perfect in their way, but they're very different. You go out unaware of your true potential, and return as fully aware Beings with all that potential realized.

Both a rock and an Archangel are essentially Light, but the rock is Light in potential and the Archangel is Light unfolded and realized. And although their essence may be identical, their function and the range and speed of their consciousness are quite different. You might give the oversight of a star system to an Archangel, but you would never assign this task to a rock!

But there is another answer to your question, and it reflects our theme in these dialogues. You begin upon this planet by working at the level of Personal Reality Creation, and have pursued that path through many lives over thousands of years. Now you are becoming aware of the next stage which is Co-Creation — and beyond that, you are beginning to get glimpses of another level: Instantaneous Creation.

Your spiritual journey is essentially the pilgrimage from Personal Reality Creation to Instantaneous Creation. This is where you are going, and this is your birthright and your destiny.

25

A Comparison Between 3D and 5D

Joanna: Could you give us some kind of comparison between our present state of consciousness and the consciousness we will experience at the fifth dimensional level?

Alariel: We will try to give you a glimpse of it, but until you experience this level of consciousness, it can only be the merest glimpse.

5D consciousness is essentially lighter, clearer, able to see more options and think more creatively than your present 3D consciousness. It is subtler, more attuned to the holistic totality of life and less involved with individual ambitions. It thinks of the highest good of all concerned, and not about personal advantage or the opportunity to acquire or gain.

The present 3D consciousness of humanity is dominated by the hopes and fears and concerns of the personality in general and the ego in particular. The ego sees no life worth having beyond its own present state of awareness, and would like to lock you into this forever, but your essential nature works against this. You have transformation written into the very fabric of your being, and you are now entering a period of rapid change. Whether the ego likes it or not, change is inevitable and is happening all around you.

The result of this change will — over time — totally alter your perspective and move you from a very limited view of life, a view imprisoned by the past, to one that is open to all possibilities. The most striking, practical change will be the

122

move from a competitive economy to a co-operative social structure, from greed and accumulation to compassion and sharing.

You're already seeing the beginning of this whenever a natural disaster hits a specific area of your planet. At that point, you abandon the principles of competitive economy, one nation vying against another, and instead you act in a way that is not in your economic interest. You mobilize help from all over the world, and pour money and resources and people and effort into trying to help the country which is suffering. So in times of crisis, you're already moving beyond the "greed and competition" scenario. When disaster strikes, you show that you understand the meaning of community in a global sense.

And it's exactly this sense of sharing and community that is now arising to save your planet from its over-competitive, consumerist nightmare. The materialist paradigm is now becoming recognized for what it is — both deeply flawed and divisive socially, and highly dangerous for the whole global environment.

So in brief, you will be moving:
from competition to co-operation,
from control to compassion,
from greed to sharing.

Your science has also been evolving, and your scientists are beginning to discover that consciousness and energy are not two separate things, but different aspects — different frequencies if you like — of one single thing. And the more powerful and developed a consciousness is, the stronger the energetic field of that person.

Here, it is a question of degree. The consciousness of the average human being is untrained, undisciplined and unfocused. It is like a diffused and weak form of light. The consciousness of a Master-soul is exactly the opposite: trained, disciplined and capable of a very exact and specific focus, like a laser beam. You can do very little with a broad and diffused beam of light, but you can do much more with a laser beam.

Comment by Stuart: Our friend Felicity Bartlett spent some time traveling with the Indian guru Swami Muktananda. She tells us that his energy-field was so powerful it set off the security scanners at airports. Here was a highly-developed consciousness which resulted in a very powerful energy-field, so powerful that it was detectable by the security equipment being used at that time.

The session with Alariel continues:

Alariel: Your science is moving on to embrace the idea of a multidimensional universe. You have found the framework of a single reality too limiting, and your brightest minds are now thinking in terms of a whole series of interconnected realities. This is where limitations start to dissolve, and many new possibilities begin to emerge.

So the big shift at the scientific level is:
from considering consciousness and energy as
two things to embracing the idea of a
single consciousness-energy continuum,
from thinking about a three dimensional world
to considering a multidimensional universe.

Science and technology have made enormous strides during the last century in the West. Within a single life-span, human beings have gone from the first powered flight to putting a manned mission on the moon — certainly a major achievement.

Yet the sad truth is that while your technology has become quite advanced, your morality has not kept pace with it. You are now in danger of becoming technological giants and moral dwarves, as the moral vacuum within your celebrity-led culture amply demonstrates.

So the big shift here will be:
from individual selfishness to social responsibility,
from exploiting the economic system to
a fair division of resources.

Yet another development lies in the recognition that, as a sentient species you are not alone in the Universe. Among the millions of galaxies, there are many sentient species, some more primitive than humanity, and some far in advance of you in both technology and the development of consciousness. Those star civilizations who have developed to an advanced level now wish to extend the hand of friendship in any way they can — or to be practical, in any way that you will allow. At present, you have a very small comfort zone when it comes to direct contact with other sentient beings, and your friends across the galaxy wish to extend the hand of friendship cautiously to avoid scaring you. So no, their spacecraft will not be landing on the White House lawn any day soon because you would find that altogether too stressful!

But through many subtle communications, signs and signals — including crop circles — they are showing you that they are there, ready and willing to help.

So here, there is a whole sequence of shifts:
from isolation to contact,
from contact to co-operation,
from co-operation to friendship.

Humanity has moved outwards to explore both your planet and a little of the space beyond it. The tide of activity has flowed out for many centuries, but now a turning point has been reached and the tide of human development is turning inwards to explore the vast reaches of consciousness. If the outer world has been rich in resources, the inner world is rich beyond your wildest imaginings.

So this is yet another shift:
from the outer to the inner,
from the world of the senses
to the world of consciousness.

Now if you put all these shifts in perception together, you will get a glimpse of what that jump from 3D to 5D will be like. But as we said, at this point it can only be a glimpse!

Joanna: The way you describe 5D consciousness, it does sound as if it will be very different from the lives most humans are experiencing now.

Alariel: Yes, very different. The 5D consciousness is lighter, gentler, more profoundly intelligent because it holds no fixed position on anything. It simply flows on and accepts everything that comes to it. In this way, it is much more balanced and resilient than most of the consciousnesses you are likely to encounter at present because the average person is so easily upset when any of their opinions or prejudices are challenged.

Being focused on Oneness, the 5D consciousness accepts the validity of all expressions of the One Life. By accepting all and condemning none, the 5D consciousness is able to float clear and free above duality. Above the need to judge and choose this as opposed to that, this person's view over that person's view. To accept all is to enter the harmony of Unity Consciousness, a state in which the mind becomes still and clear and full of Light.

All this may seem mind-bendingly modern to many people, but actually the Master-souls of humanity have been thinking about these things for centuries. They may have used other labels and called it "non-duality" or "the Real" rather than "5D consciousness," but they were talking about the same thing.

Joanna: And will 5D consciousness affect everything in our lives, even down to the small things?

Alariel: Yes. Let us take a practical example here, and consider how people read books. At present, they may speed-read, but with 5D consciousness you can read books in quite a different way, by focusing on their energy. Every non-fiction book has a number of ideas in it. Most books only have a few ideas in them, and everything else is just commentary and padding. When the writer starts to talk directly about ideas, the energy of the text changes, and a well-tuned consciousness can detect this change in energy. Ideas focus consciousness into a faster and more free-flowing stream of energy, so partly, you're picking up the change of pace involved.

By attuning to the pace of the energy in the text, you can sense when ideas are starting to emerge and focus on them. When the idea has been presented, the pace slows down again, and you can skip all the slow-moving material because it's ideas-free. Working your way through a book in this way, you can read and absorb the ideas and leave the rest — a much more effective process than speed-reading.

Joanna: And will all these changes affect how we perceive the world around us?

Alariel: Certainly. You will become more aware of living in a multi-faceted Universe. Your brightest minds have already started thinking in terms of many dimensions. Once this point has been reached, many other breakthroughs become possible. One of the biggest of these is the shifting of ascension from the realm of religion to the realm of science. When you start thinking of ascension as a transition from the third to the fifth dimension, you're ready to see the process of human transformation with new eyes. If ascension is just stepping into the next dimensional reality, you can begin to understand it as a stage in the ongoing process of expanding your consciousness.

Most human beings operate within a very narrow band of consciousness, staying inside what you could almost describe as a single frequency-group or "color" of awareness. That approach is now getting more difficult to sustain, and you're being challenged to move out into other frequency-groups and operate on several levels at the same time. This is all preparing you for the big leap into focusing across the full gamut of all frequency-groups, embracing all the colors in what could be called Full-Spectrum Consciousness or Rainbow Consciousness.

Any consciousness smaller than this inevitably distorts and limits the Truth, simply because there are aspects of Truth that it cannot see. Rainbow Consciousness marks a shift from considering your individual good to considering the good of all concerned, and we don't just mean human beings, but animals, plants, crystals and the whole of Gaia too.

Joanna: Are there any physical indications, signs in the body, that would show us we're getting close to Rainbow Consciousness?

Alariel: Yes. As you approach Rainbow Consciousness, there are physical changes that signal something different is happening. Your mind feels clearer, sharper, able to perceive a whole raft of subtle things you weren't aware of before, and there is also a change in your field of vision. Your whole field of vision opens up so that you can see more of the landscape in front of you, both horizontally and vertically. To use one of the phrases from your culture, we could say that it's as if the movie of your life has suddenly gone into widescreen.

Joanna: And the whole quality of the consciousness changes too?
Alariel: Of course. Rainbow Consciousness can see many more possibilities, options and combinations, so that makes it very much more creative than your present awareness. However, dealing with such a broad creative menu of possibilities may be challenging at first for a mind that has been used to a simpler range of options. Rainbow Consciousness needs a lighter touch, and the ability to deal with subtler signals than you've been used to. Some of these signals may be personal, but some will link you into the consciousness of Gaia, and others will resonate with the full range of galaxies, the whole cosmic environment in which you live. This will be very different from the way you receive consciousness-input now, and it will be more like a form of multi-tasking, but in this case it could be called Cosmic Multi-Tasking or CMT!

What we have already said about the evolution of the channeling process is relevant here. When a full awareness conscious channel starts to weave strands of consciousness together, some from his or her channeling source and some from interaction with the people he or she is talking to in a workshop, they are starting to operate in this CMT way. That is only the first level of this skill. And the more you are able to deal with a whole raft of subtle signals, the more exciting and stimulating the CMT mix is going to be.

It's going to take a whole range of new skills to handle this new sensitivity, but the really skilled people in this field will seem like virtuosi. Many of them will be Crystal Children, and they will be Virtuosi with Consciousness! Not only will they be able to deal with subtle signals from across the galaxy, and pull down answers instantly, but they will be operating at what will seem to you to be prodigious speed. When Rainbow Consciousness is being used effectively, it can't help being a whole lot faster than the kind of mental processes you're used to. And this rapidity is not hyper-activity, it is not dysfunctional in any way. It's light and easy and in total control — but it IS fast! It will be like watching a musical virtuoso performing at incredible speed.

And that's really the whole point: consciousness IS an instrument, but an instrument of such power, range, subtlety and flexibility that most human beings now living will not be able to grasp the full extent of its potential.

This whole process of opening up your consciousness and developing new skills is part of your overall unfolding and empowerment. And as you begin to see the extent of your expanded Being, you will also recognize that your time is coming.

In the past, you have sat at the feet
of great teachers like Jeshua,
Mother Mary and Mary Magdalene,
and now it 's your turn to teach and to lead,
your turn to inspire the next wave of teachers
as they awaken and discover
the power of the Light within them.

26

Beyond Limitation

Alariel: The whole process of living on the Earth is teaching you to master your limitations, and move on into much higher frequencies of consciousness and being. When a thing seems impossible, remember that it's only impossible on your present level of consciousness. By empowering your consciousness, you can push back the boundaries of the possible:

If you can shift your consciousness
onto a high enough level,
and use the energies
available at that level,
there is nothing you cannot do.

When you realize that, and start to live from that understanding, you will be able to transcend the limitations which have restricted you for so long. This is all part of the process of waking up to who you are and accepting a new level of empowerment.

Joanna: It's not always easy to stay in our power here, with so many influences trying to keep us small and controllable.

Alariel: Yes, agreed. After many lifetimes in a veiled state, you have persuaded yourselves that you are beings with very little power, but the truth is very different: you are wise and powerful Beings of Light. When you attune to the Light, you begin to see that the only limitations in your life are those that you have created. And once created, these limitations only endure because you continue to accept them. If you stand strong in your own truth and deny their power over you, they will vanish like the morning mist at the rising of the sun.

In this new empowerment, you will be able to see and accept your past lives within a much broader framework, and be able to acknowledge the whole truth about your past:

In your past lives most of you have had
a broad spectrum of experience,
and you have been
the good and the bad,
the beautiful and the ugly,
the mystics and the warriors,
the priests and the rebels,
the heroes and the villains.
And the challenge is to look beyond
the limiting dualities,
and accept all of it,
without going into judgment.

Seeing your past lives within this broader and more accepting framework is part of your adjustment to these times of rapid change. In times of change, there are many opportunities to go beyond your present limitations and make a fresh start on a higher and clearer level of consciousness. This will bring major changes not only into your lives, but the lives of all those around you. Some of these people may be frightened of change, and will try to resist it. The people who fight against change may cling to past experiences, familiar patterns and old possessions, and draw comfort from the word "forever."

But from our perspective, nothing in the Universe exists forever because change is the great constant within all life. Even the Universe itself does not last forever. It was born out of the Void, out of Great Mystery, and one day it will return to Great Mystery and cease to be. That is why the word "forever" has no meaning for us.

Some people think that Truth can be "forever," but we perceive it differently. For us, Truth is continuously evolving, refining and expanding. Let me give you an example of what we mean. When the Master Djwhal Khul was working with Alice Bailey in the early years of the twentieth century, he presented the information on the Rays — that is, the universal structure of energy-quality — as essentially sevenfold. There is now an opening up of information on the Ray system so that it can be seen in a much broader way, with information on new Rays being brought out into human awareness.

This evolution of information on the Rays is an entirely natural process, and these new developments do not displace or devalue the original information. However, they do open up higher octaves of understanding, and these were too subtle and advanced to be communicated at an earlier stage.

Comment by Stuart: Our friend Sue Fraser, helped by the international channel Paul McCarthy, is channeling a new understanding of the Rays called the "Rays of Emergence System." This is fast developing into a powerful technique for self-development, self-healing and transformation. Sue may be contacted through her website: www.intuitionandrays.co.uk. Paul McCarthy's website is: www.siriusascension.com.

27

Learning and Growing

Alariel: There is another way you can look at the creative process, and that is to see it in terms of learning and growing.

There are two main ways of learning: learning through joy and learning through pain.

Joy is light, joy is loving, and it naturally moves into co-operation and sharing, and expresses itself in flow and change. Joy sees the whole world as safe and open, and full of new friends and opportunities to spread love and happiness.

Pain is heavy, pain is resentful, and it naturally moves into competition and greed, and expresses itself in rigid structures and resistance to change. Pain sees the whole world as threatening, and puts a lot of effort into issues of safety and security.

Whether you choose to learn and grow through joy, or through pain, you will still be learning, but the path of joy leads to rapid progress towards the Light, while the path of pain has many dead-ends and twists and turns in it.

It is also easy to fall asleep spiritually upon the path of pain because progress is so slow and there is very little forward momentum. The whole process of reality creation works best when there is change and flow and movement in the consciousness because then the whole life experience will have a certain momentum about it. The most important thing about this momentum is that it helps you to keep awake spiritually. Flow, change and movement are qualities at the heart of the Universe, and it naturally resonates with any consciousness that moves and flows.

If you wish to take advantage of the optimum energy-wave of reality creation, to surf the wave of Universal Being, then the qualities to develop in your life and your consciousness are flow, movement and openness to change.

The more accepting, flowing and open-to-change you make your consciousness, the more the forces of reality creation will work for you, and the faster you will move beyond any limitation that restricts the effectiveness of your creative process.

Out of all the information in these dialogues, one key fact emerges: that reality creation mirrors the levels in human consciousness. Because reality creation echoes the structure of human consciousness, you can see how the creative process, extended over time, takes you deeper and deeper into your own being.

Through the process of manifesting a reality, and learning how to make that reality better and better, you steadily change and grow. It is this which makes the creative process such an essential part of your life and your development:

Creating a better reality
is not just something that you do,
a skill that you exercise,
it's the way you learn and grow
as human beings.

The principles emerging at this universal level demonstrate the central importance of the creative process to an understanding of the human condition. And it would be difficult to reach a full understanding of human potential and the way that human development is supported by the Universe without first understanding how reality is created.

What is emerging from these dialogues is a level of insight into the foundations of the creative process. These foundations reveal the way reality creation is intermeshed with human consciousness and human development, an interconnection that can be summarized in three Fundamental Principles of Reality Creation:

1 Through creating a better reality, you learn and grow.
2 The levels of the creative process mirror the structure of human consciousness.
3 Through manifesting a series of realities, you journey deeper into your own being.

At their deepest level, the processes of reality creation serve you in your quest for self-knowledge and self-realization. They are central to your inner journey and the way in which you unfold your powers and manifest your consciousness.

28

The Arc of Spiritual Development

Joanna: Have we seen only a small part of human potential so far?

Alariel: It is very difficult for someone focusing at the personality level to get any idea of the vastness of human development. Yes, they can draw back and look at the bigger picture when the soul is in the Interlife and the next life is being planned, but due to the veiling process, this information does not filter down directly to the personality in the next incarnation. The personality may have glimpses of it from time to time in the form of dreams, visions, flashes of clarity and insight, but for many people, these moments of clarity are too brief to give them consistent and reliable guidance, or to develop the sense of an underlying purpose for their lives.

This is where an understanding of reality creation can prove its value. When you understand that your process of reality creation fits within the overall arc of your spiritual development, this knowledge can help you to make sense of your life. If you are at the personality level, still working with the ego, then Personal Reality Creation will be the only way you wish to create your reality. But as you move towards focusing upon the soul, you will feel attracted by the idea of Co-Creation. Even this is only a stage upon your journey, for as you start to focus strongly on the higher self, you will feel drawn towards the process of Instantaneous Creation.

The arc of your spiritual development as multi-dimensional Beings is vast, and at this stage, you will be able to perceive only a tiny portion of the unfoldment that is to come. But even now you can glimpse the broad sweep of your Being, from the grounding of the physical body to the soaring aspiration of the higher self.

When you think of this bigger picture, you begin to see your life on Earth in a different way. Your life becomes endowed with a deeper meaning as part of the process of learning and growing, a cycle of development that gives purpose to your whole existence.

Despite all the limitations that seem to press in around you, you are in fact spiritual Beings rooted in the Greater Reality of the Universe. That overall structure makes transformation inevitable, as you move onwards through your arc of unfoldment as multidimensional Children of the Light.

When you glimpse this great arc of your spiritual development and realize that it runs parallel with the Transition of the Earth, you begin to understand the real significance of this special time. Yes, 2012 is part of it, but only a part, and as you expand your consciousness, you will be able to go on and explore all the possibilities of being.

Now is the time for you to awaken,
set aside the veil of forgetting
and put off the cloak of limitation.
Now is the time to stand up
in Love and Power,
and let your Light shine.

Part Seven:

Conclusion

29

An Emerging Understanding

Joanna: Why do you think we have been unable to understand reality creation for so long?

Alariel: Partly because you have put things into little self-contained boxes and have failed to see the connections between these boxes. Although we have divided our analysis into a number of components, we have been careful to show the connections between these components, so that you can understand the whole process of reality creation.

Another big impediment to understanding reality creation has been the assumption that this process must be governed by rigid laws that do not distinguish one person from another. As you have seen in the case of Personal Reality Creation, the governing Principles are modified by Limiting Protocols which have the effect of personalizing the Basic Mechanism, and tailoring it to the specific situation of the individual. It is only by grasping the combination of universal principles and individual modifications that a real understanding of the whole process can start to emerge.

Joanna: Are there other ways of approaching this process and analyzing it?

Alariel: We have discussed the process of reality creation at the level of concepts, but of course there are a number of ways in which this process can be analyzed. In addition to what we have discussed here, there is a physics, a chemistry, and a biology of reality creation. However, we will not be addressing these aspects because other groups are already well advanced in their research upon them, and a start has been made in presenting some of this information.

You stand now at the very beginning of the study of reality creation in an organized way. To make rapid progress in this area, you will need to develop a whole language and vocabulary of reality creation before the deeper and more subtle areas can be communicated by this, or any other group.

There is a parallel here with the study of time. When you first began to explore the theory of timelines, you had no language to express the subtle interactions of timelines and the fluid ebb and flow of time-energies. The possibility of time-paradoxes then opened up for you, and you began to explore subtle areas of process and logic that could never have been understood by your ancestors, for whom time was a rigid structure underpinning a linear and predictable Universe.

Now you can look back at your ancestors' perception of time with all the advantages of a developed logic and a rich and subtle vocabulary attuned to the expression of that logic. This will be exactly the position of your descendants when they consider the field of reality creation. They will have developed the logic, the concepts, the vocabulary needed to understand this subject in all its subtlety and complexity.

Joanna: And is there one key aspect of reality creation which stands out and has special significance?

Alariel: Yes. Out of all the information on this subject, one key fact emerges: that reality creation mirrors the levels in human consciousness. Because reality creation runs parallel with human consciousness, you can see how the creative process, extended over time, takes you deeper and deeper into your own being. That journey of self-realization is paralleled by the development of a greater understanding of the Universe and the way reality is created within it. And through understanding the whole spectrum of reality creation, you begin to understand your own nature, and the full extent of human potential.

30

Summation

When we started work on this project, we had been in dialogue with Alariel for over a year during the production of our second book. His involvement had transformed our research and enabled us to explore the background to the female disciples of Jeshua, and the real significance of Mary Magdalene. We knew his group worked closely with the Order of Melchizedek, and as the Melchizedeks had strong links with the Essenes, we were in a sense prepared for his knowledge and expertise in that area.

However, the creation of personal reality is quite a different field of enquiry, and when we began asking about this, we had no idea what his response might be. Would he claim ignorance of this subject and advise us to consult another source? Or would he offer only a superficial understanding of how reality is created? As it turned out, he did neither of these things, and the depth of his knowledge and the confident way he handled our questions both surprised and delighted us.

After setting this project in motion, we watched it unfold, and as the process continued, our respect for Alariel steadily grew. He was never afraid to tackle the tough questions, and his approach was always logical and precise. We came to recognize a cool and balanced quality about Alariel's consciousness, as if he was looking down over the whole landscape of reality creation, seeing the connections between the different aspects, and describing them with detached precision.

When at last the channeling process was complete, we could look back and see the project as a whole, and test it with searching questions:

Does it advance our knowledge in this area?
Is the information consistent?
How much of it is new?
How far does it go beyond what is already known?
And what does all this really amount to?

Having reviewed the information, there was one obvious conclusion:

What Alariel has presented here
is a new understanding of life.

Alariel perceives reality creation as mirroring the levels in human consciousness, so that as the creative process extends over time, it takes us deeper into our own being. And he places the process of creating reality within the span of our development, so that we can see both where we have come from — Personal Reality Creation, and where we are going — Co-Creation, and eventually even Instantaneous Creation. But more than this — he also identifies reality creation as central to our development, the one key process through which we learn and grow.

In addition, Alariel's perspective connects our shift in consciousness with the Transition of the Earth. He links reality creation into the 2012 experience and projects our imagination beyond that into a new world and a new consciousness.

The more that consciousness develops, and the deeper we go into the creative process, the more we understand ourselves and our own potential. Alariel describes this journey of exploration in these words:

You are constantly being challenged
to expand your awareness
and reach out into
new frequencies of consciousness,
new perspectives of truth,
new possibilities of being.

Further Reading

Arntz, William; Chasse, Betsy; and Vicente, Mark, *What the Bleep Do We Know: Discovering the endless possibilities for altering your everyday reality*, Health Communications, Deerfield Beach, FL, 2005. A stimulating book that brings together science and spirituality in the exploration of personal reality.

Braden, Gregg, *Awakening to Zero Point*, Radio Bookstore Press, Bellevue, WA, 1997. A helpful guide to the science underlying the Transition of the Earth and the change in consciousness.

Braden, Gregg, *The Divine Matrix: Bridging time, space, miracles and belief*, Hay House, Carlsbad, CA, 2007. A remarkable book connecting consciousness and the creation of reality with the latest developments in science.

Byrne, Rhonda, *The Secret*, Simon & Schuster, London, 2006. A well-presented survey of ideas within the basic mechanism of reality creation.

Cooper, Diana, *A Little Light on the Spiritual Laws*, Hodder & Stoughton, London, 2000. The best general introduction to the whole field of Universal Law.

Cooper, Diana, *A New Light on Ascension*, Findhorn Press, Forres, Scotland, 2004. An updated version of *A Little Light on Ascension*, with 12 new chapters. This is the clearest and most practical general survey of Ascension for the beginner.

Cooper, Diana, *A Time for Transformation: How to awaken to your soul's purpose and claim your power*, Piatkus, London 1992. An inspirational book about changing the way we live.

Edwards, Gill, *Living Magically*, Piatkus, London, 1991. The first of a series of books that present a new vision of Reality. These books are practical, easy to read and full of clarity and insight.

Gawain, Shakti, *The Path of Transformation: How Healing Ourselves Can Change the World*, Nataraj Publishing, Mill Valley, CA, 1993. Offers a clear understanding of the process of change and transformation, and practical ways to support it.

Gerard, Robert, *Change Your DNA, Change Your Life!* Oughten House Foundation, Coarsegold, CA, 2000. A practical system for transforming ourselves at the physical and psychological levels.

Hay, Louise, *You Can Heal Your Life*, Hay House, Carlsbad, CA, 1984. A book which courageously extended and developed the principles first channeled by Seth, and applied them to help people find self-esteem and self-love. This classic text remains an inspiration to many people all over the world.

Hicks, Esther and Jerry, *The Law of Attraction: How to Make it Work for You*, Hay House, Carlsbad, CA, 2006. A wise and practical book which presents the Teachings of the channeling source called Abraham.

Holbeche, Soozi, *Changes: A Guide to Personal Transformation and New Ways of Living in the Next Millennium*, Piatkus, London, 1997. A book full of clarity and down-to-earth ideas to help us manage the process of change.

Hurtak, J. J, *The Book of Knowledge: The Keys of Enoch*, The Academy For Future Science, Los Gatos, CA, 1973. A profound text which is widely regarded as the ultimate source-book on the relationship between consciousness and the multidimensional universe. The DVD-video Merkabah: Voyage of a Star Seed by Dr. Hurtak and Jean-Luc Bozzoli gives a visual overview of this material.

Mohr, Barbel, *The Cosmic Ordering Service*, Hodder & Stoughton, London, 2006. A simple account of the essence of the basic mechanism, without going into the detail of the process.

Ramtha, *A Beginner's Guide to Creating Reality*, (channeled by J.Z. Knight), J.Z.K. Publishing, Yelm, WA, 1998. A new understanding of the fabric of reality and how it is connected with the mind and the brain.

Redfield, James, and Adrienne, Carol, *The Celestine Prophecy: An Experiential Guide*, Bantam, London, 1995. A useful and thorough companion volume to the inspirational bestseller, *The Celestine Prophecy*.

Schucman, Helen, *A Course in Miracles*, Foundation for Inner Peace, Mill Valley, CA, 1975 (second edition Viking Penguin, London, 1996.) A self-study course channeled by Helen Schucman: it is designed to help in changing perceptions. This book is widely recognized as one of the great classics of 20th century channeling.

Seale, Alan, *The Manifestation Wheel: A Practical Process for Creating Miracles*, Weiser Books, San Francisco, CA, 2008. An interesting eightfold process to turn the theory of manifestation into practical reality.

Seth, *The Nature of Personal Reality*, (channeled by Jane Roberts), New World Library, Novato, CA, 1974. A classic text which has been an inspiration to many people. Back in the 1970s no one was focusing on these things, till Seth came along and changed all that. A few books — a very few — can be said to have changed the world. This is one of them.

Spangler, David, *The Laws of Manifestation*, Findhorn Publications, Forres, Scotland, 1976. Based on the author's work with the Findhorn Community during the 1970s. This is the book which first focused on the concept of "manifesting" and brought it to popular attention. The fourfold process described in this book has some parallels with Alariel's perception of Co-Creation.

Vallee, Martine (Editor), *The Great Shift: Co-Creating a New World for 2012 and Beyond*, Weiser Books, San Francisco, CA, 2009. Some remarkable channeling by Lee Carroll, Tom Kenyon and Patricia Cori.

Wilson, Stuart, and Prentis, Joanna, *Power of the Magdalene*, Ozark Mountain Publishing, Huntsville, AR, 2009. Based on past life regression with seven subjects. This is our second book, containing a lot more information about the female disciples of Jeshua, and a whole section on the New Children, especially the Crystal Children. This book also describes our first contact with Alariel.

Note: Some of the books cited above (especially the more esoteric titles) may be difficult to source from general bookshops. They can be obtained from Arcturus Books at www.arcturusbooks.co.uk, phone 01803 864363, from Aristia at www.aristia.co.uk, phone 01983 721060, or from Cygnus at www.cygnus-books.co.uk, phone 01550 777701.

Acknowledgments

We would like to thank Gill Edwards for her inspiring workshops and helpful books: these first focused our interest on how we create our reality.

We would like to say a big "thank you" to the whole Ozark publishing team, especially Dolores Cannon and Julia Degan, for their care and creativity in the production of this book.

151

Other Books by Stuart Wilson and Joanna Prentis

The Essenes, Children of the Light

The inner story of the Essene Brotherhood, seen from the past life perspective of Daniel, an Essene elder, and his friend Joseph of Arimathea. Tells the dramatic story of Jesus' healing in the tomb and reveals Essene links with the Druids and the Order of Melchizedek.

Power of the Magdalene

A blend of the past life experiences of seven subjects and channeling by Alariel. Reveals the existence of a group of female disciples, and the real significance of Mary Magdalene as the spiritual partner of Jeshua. Contains a whole section on the New Children who are now being born.

About the Authors

Joanna Prentis: I was born in Bangalore in southern India. When I was nearly three, my family returned to Scotland where I spent my childhood and teenage years. After leaving school, I traveled extensively, married and lived in Hong Kong for two years and then ten years in the bush in Western Australia, where my three daughters were born. It was there that my interest began in alternative medicine and education, organic farming, metaphysics and meditation. With a local nurse, we ran a Homeopathic and Radionic practice.

I returned to the UK in 1979 and later trained as a Montessori teacher, educating my two youngest daughters, Katinka and Larissa, at home for a few years. I now have three beautiful grandchildren.

I did several healing courses and have a foundation diploma in Humanistic Psychology. I also trained with Ursula Markham and have a diploma in Hypnotherapy and Past Life Therapy.

With my eldest daughter Tatanya, I set up the Starlight Centre in 1988, a centre for healing and the expansion of consciousness. Over the years, Tatanya has introduced us to many innovative techniques and interesting people.

In 1999 we closed the Centre to focus on producing our books. I continue with my Past Life work, and readers now connect with us from all over the world.

You can visit Joanna at her website:
www.foundationforcrystalchildren.com

Stuart Wilson is a writer on new perspectives whose perceptions have been developed through 30 years of working with groups committed to personal growth. For nine years, Stuart co-focalized (with Joanna Prentis) the Starlight Centre in the West of England, a centre dedicated to healing and the transformation of consciousness.

He writes about this period:

"It was inspiring and fascinating but also exhausting! A stream of visitors came in to the Centre, mainly from the United States and Australia, but some also from Europe. We had an amazing and mind-bending time sitting at the feet of internationally respected spiritual teachers and workshop leaders."

Part of the work of the Centre was research into past lives, and this led to his collaboration with Joanna to write *The Essenes, Children of the Light* and *Power of the Magdalene*, both published by Ozark Mountain Publishing

You can visit Stuart at his website:
www.foundationforcrystalchildren.com

Other Books by Ozark Mountain Publishing, Inc.

Dolores Cannon
A Soul Remembers Hiroshima
Between Death and Life
Conversations with Nostradamus,
    Volume I, II, III
The Convoluted Universe -Book One,
    Two, Three, Four, Five
The Custodians
Five Lives Remembered
Jesus and the Essenes
Keepers of the Garden
Legacy from the Stars
The Legend of Starcrash
The Search for Hidden Sacred Knowledge
They Walked with Jesus
The Three Waves of Volunteers and the
    New Earth
Aron Abrahamsen
Holiday in Heaven
Out of the Archives – Earth Changes
James Ream Adams
Little Steps
Justine Alessi & M. E. McMillan
Rebirth of the Oracle
Kathryn/Patrick Andries
Naked in Public
Kathryn Andries
The Big Desire
Dream Doctor
Soul Choices: Six Paths to Find Your Life
    Purpose
Soul Choices: Six Paths to Fulfilling
    Relationships
Patrick Andries
Owners Manual for the Mind
Cat Baldwin
Divine Gifts of Healing
Dan Bird
Finding Your Way in the Spiritual Age
Waking Up in the Spiritual Age
Julia Cannon
Soul Speak – The Language of Your Body
Ronald Chapman
Seeing True
Albert Cheung
The Emperor's Stargate
Jack Churchward
Lifting the Veil on the Lost Continent of
    Mu
The Stone Tablets of Mu
Sherri Cortland

Guide Group Fridays
Raising Our Vibrations for the New Age
Spiritual Tool Box
Windows of Opportunity
Patrick De Haan
The Alien Handbook
Paulinne Delcour-Min
Spiritual Gold
Holly Ice
Divine Fire
Joanne DiMaggio
Edgar Cayce and the Unfulfilled Destiny
    of Thomas Jefferson Reborn
Anthony DeNino
The Power of Giving and Gratitude
Michael Dennis
Morning Coffee with God
God's Many Mansions
Carolyn Greer Daly
Opening to Fullness of Spirit
Anita Holmes
Twidders
Aaron Hoopes
Reconnecting to the Earth
Victoria Hunt
Kiss the Wind
Patricia Irvine
In Light and In Shade
Kevin Killen
Ghosts and Me
Diane Lewis
From Psychic to Soul
Donna Lynn
From Fear to Love
Maureen McGill
Baby It's You
Maureen McGill & Nola Davis
Live from the Other Side
Curt Melliger
Heaven Here on Earth
Henry Michaelson
And Jesus Said – A Conversation
Dennis Milner
Kosmos
Andy Myers
Not Your Average Angel Book
Guy Needler
Avoiding Karma
Beyond the Source – Book 1, Book 2
The Anne Dialogues

For more information about any of the above titles, soon to be released titles,
or other items in our catalog, write, phone or visit our website:
PO Box 754, Huntsville, AR 72740
479-738-2348/800-935-0045
www.ozarkmt.com

Other Books by Ozark Mountain Publishing, Inc.

The Curators
The History of God
The Origin Speaks
James Nussbaumer
And Then I Knew My Abundance
The Master of Everything
Mastering Your Own Spiritual Freedom
Living Your Dram, Not Someone Else's
Sherry O'Brian
Peaks and Valleys
Riet Okken
The Liberating Power of Emotions
Gabrielle Orr
Akashic Records: One True Love
Let Miracles Happen
Victor Parachin
Sit a Bit
Nikki Pattillo
A Spiritual Evolution
Children of the Stars
Rev. Grant H. Pealer
A Funny Thing Happened on the
    Way to Heaven
Worlds Beyond Death
Victoria Pendragon
Born Healers
Feng Shui from the Inside, Out
Sleep Magic
The Sleeping Phoenix
Being In A Body
Michael Perlin
Fantastic Adventures in Metaphysics
Walter Pullen
Evolution of the Spirit
Debra Rayburn
Let's Get Natural with Herbs
Charmian Redwood
A New Earth Rising
Coming Home to Lemuria
David Rivinus
Always Dreaming
Richard Rowe
Imagining the Unimaginable
Exploring the Divine Library
M. Don Schorn
Elder Gods of Antiquity
Legacy of the Elder Gods
Gardens of the Elder Gods
Reincarnation...Stepping Stones of Life
Garnet Schulhauser

Dance of Eternal Rapture
Dance of Heavenly Bliss
Dancing Forever with Spirit
Dancing on a Stamp
Manuella Stoerzer
Headless Chicken
Annie Stillwater Gray
Education of a Guardian Angel
The Dawn Book
Work of a Guardian Angel
Joys of a Guardian Angel
Blair Styra
Don't Change the Channel
Who Catharted
Natalie Sudman
Application of Impossible Things
L.R. Sumpter
Judy's Story
The Old is New
We Are the Creators
Artur Tradevosyan
Croton
Jim Thomas
Tales from the Trance
Jolene and Jason Tierney
A Quest of Transcendence
Nicholas Vesey
Living the Life-Force
Janie Wells
Embracing the Human Journey
Payment for Passage
Dennis Wheatley/ Maria Wheatley
The Essential Dowsing Guide
Maria Wheatley
Druidic Soul Star Astrology
Jacquelyn Wiersma
The Zodiac Recipe
Sherry Wilde
The Forgotten Promise
Lyn Willmoth
A Small Book of Comfort
Stuart Wilson & Joanna Prentis
Atlantis and the New Consciousness
Beyond Limitations
The Essenes -Children of the Light
The Magdalene Version
Power of the Magdalene
Robert Winterhalter
The Healing Christ

For more information about any of the above titles, soon to be released titles,
or other items in our catalog, write, phone or visit our website:
PO Box 754, Huntsville, AR 72740
479-738-2348/800-935-0045
www.ozarkmt.com

Made in the USA
Thornton, CO
05/13/22 13:30:33

b6525782-d8a6-4fc4-8bd5-58997700a548R01